MW00417118

Meditations
from
The School of Jesus Crucified

From the Italian of Father Ignatius of the Side of
Jesus, Passionist

Published originally 1866

republished by Jacob Stein,
student of the theology faculty at the Pontifical
University of Saint Thomas at Rome,

founder of Filii Passionis,

and

author of the blog
www.PassioXP.com

2018

TABLE OF CONTENTS

Introduction   i

Day 1 – Jesus Christ takes leave of His
    Blessed Mother   1

Day 2 – Jesus is sold by Judas Iscariot   9

Day 3 – Prayer of Jesus in the Garden   18

Day 4 – The Agony and bloody Sweat of
    Jesus in the Garden of Olives   24

Day 5 – Jesus is betrayed with a Kiss by
    Judas   29

Day 6 – Jesus is taken and bound by the
    Soldiers   34

Day 7 – Jesus is led before the Tribunal of
    Annas   39

Day 8 – Jesus receives a Blow   45

Day 9 – Jesus before Caiaphas   51

Day 10 – Jesus Christ is denied by St. Peter   57

Day 11 – Jesus is derided and treated most
    ignominiously in the House of
    Caiaphas   63

Day 12 – Jesus is led before Pilate, the
    Roman Governor   69

Day 13 – Jesus before the Tribunal of Pilate   76

Day 14 – Jesus is presented before Herod   82

Day 15 – Barabbas preferred before Jesus   89

Day 16 – Jesus scourged at the Pillar   95

Day 17 – Jesus is crowned with Thorns   101

Day 18 – Jesus Christ shown by Pilate to the

People   108

Day 19 – Jesus condemned to the Death of
the Cross   115

Day 20 – Jesus carries His Cross to Mount
Calvary   122

Day 21 – The Meeting between Jesus and
His blessed Mother   130

Day 22 – The pious Women lament over
Jesus   137

Day 23 – Jesus is assisted by Simon of
Cyrene to bear the Cross   144

Day 24 – Jesus nailed to the Cross   152

Day 25 – Jesus elevated on His Cross in the
sight of all   160

Day 26 – Jesus Crucified prays for His
Enemies   168

Day 27 – Jesus from His Cross bestows
Mary upon us as our Mother   176

Day 28 – Jesus Crucified complains of being
forsaken by His Eternal Father   184

Day 29 – Thirst of Jesus on the Cross   191

Day 30 – Jesus dies on the Cross   198

Day 31 – The Side of Jesus wounded by a
Spear   205

INTRODUCTION

It would be proper to begin with the words of Saint Paul of the Cross:

> *On awaking, keep your heart under control, by the remembrance of God, your Love, your only Good. When God inspires you with a sentiment of love, stop and taste it, as the bee sips the honey. Ah! when I reflect that my soul is the temple of God, that God dwells in me, how my heart rejoices! All sufferings and afflictions appear to me sweet and light. What a fruitful source of meditation! Live in the joy and the peace of the divine Majesty. Live lost in divine love. Live for divine love and of divine love. Oh cherished cross! Through thee my most bitter trials are replete with graces!*

Following these words should remind us the simplicity with which we should enter in to prayer. We live in an age where everything has seemed to become overcomplicated. It better be new and flashy or its liable to be thrown aside. And for those who are striving to follow Christ each day, we sometimes end our days shaking our head and wondering why we cannot communicate to the world how great of a gift we have been given in Faith, that is, Jesus Himself! Jesus Crucified, for love of you and me!

The world is worn out, exhausted from our arguments and our disputations and presentations and conferences. Our arguments are not working. The world is not interested in our words. One last resort remains: holiness.

Holiness will be the only thing that will move hearts to conversion in this day and age. One could say this is the new approach that should be taken in communicating Christ to the world, but, in reality, it is the perennial approach. The tried and true approach, as many Saints have attested to, is devotion to the Passion, first, for the certainty of our own salvation, second, to grow in all the virtues Christ lived perfectly, and eminently so in His Passion. It will be only from such a vantage point that we will be able to move hearts towards Christ.

Begin with prayer. A wise and loving priest once instructed that I should spend 15 minutes a day at the Foot of the Cross. And that, in this short span of time, I should present to Christ everything! Everything of myself, everything of what Christ did for me, everything! Every joy, every hope, every care, every anxiety, every gratitude, every fear. Nothing should be held back before Christ and what more fitting place to tell Him than at the Foot of the Cross as He expresses His Thirst for me. This is the most profound relationship we can ever have on this earth and that we will ever be able to participate in throughout all eternity.

This is how simple prayer should be. We only have to make the time for it. This book of meditations is meant to form the Christian reader in the sentiments and affections of the Gospel. It follows the story of the Passion of Christ as presented to us in the Scriptures and faithfully presents to us objects of meditation from which much fruit can be gained in our spiritual life. Prayer should be simple, but that does not mean it will be easy. The first step will be humility and the second to follow quickly after will need to be perseverance.

* * * * *

This devotional is presented by a group of Roman Catholic laymen aspiring to live a traditional monastic life according to the Rule of Saint Paul of the Cross. At the moment, the men do not live in community. It is their prayer that this will come to fruition soon for the sake of the glorification of God, their sanctification, the sanctification of others and the assistance of Holy Mother Church.

The prayers and sacrifices of these men are united to this Holy Rule of their father, Saint Paul of the Cross. According to their circumstances, they strive to apply the maxims of this Rule to daily life. In your charity, please pray for this endeavor of reform.

The devout inspiration of this group is the patrimony of Saint Paul of the Cross. This group of men will gather inspired as Saint Mary Magdalene was prior to the Passion of Our Blessed Lord. It was she who gave example of how we should make reparation to Christ, Who in His Passion was spat upon, beaten, scourged, mocked. She understood, having turned from a life of sin by the gentle voice of Our Lord. She, with great sorrow for her sins, anointed our Lord's Head with precious ointment and bathed His Feet with her tears, knowing that His Love would move Him to lay down His life for her, for you. So men must gather to do the same, to make reparation to Our Blessed Lord for the sins of mankind, for their own sins, and come to know ever more deeply the Love of Christ in His Passion, in His Crucifixion, so that they may be led, and lead souls, to the glory of the Resurrection!

Saint Gemma is also a particular patroness of this endeavor. It is she who is called, in death, foundress of the Passionist monastery at Lucca, though the very order refused her entry, in life. She is a perennial model, but is a model especially for our times. Her love for the Passion and her love for the Blessed Sacrament were one and the same. Jesus in the Eucharist and Jesus on the Cross would be throughout Gemma's life the inseparable objects of her love. Sons of the Passion must gather also as sons of the Most Blessed Sacrament. They will love Christ in the Blessed Sacrament, the Gift given the night before He was betrayed. They will make reparation for this betrayal and for the lack of love and the many sacrileges and profanations against our Adorable Lord in the Blessed Sacrament. They will love Christ in the Eucharist, they will love Christ on the Cross!

May this work bear fruit in your spiritual life, in growing ever more profoundly in love with Love Crucified, through a greater encounter with the constant thought of you by Christ in His Life and in His Passion! In all things, He thought of you!

Our Lady of Sorrows, pray for us!
Saint Paul of the Cross, pray for us!
Saint John, brother of Paul, pray for us!
Saint Gabriel of Our Lady of Sorrows, pray for us!
Saint Mary Magdalene, pray for us!
Saint Gemma, pray for us!

In vulneribus Christi,

Jacob Stein

12 February 2018
Feast of the Seven Founders
of the Servite Order

iv

Preparation for Meditation

*In the Name + of the Father, and of the Son,
and the Holy Ghost. Amen.*

My sweet Lord, I thank Thee for having
suffered so much, and for having died on
the Cross for love of me. Most amiable
Redeemer, through the merits of Thy
Passion, save my soul. Amen.

*Recollecting that you are in the Presence of
God,*

Say three *Our Fathers* in memory of His
bitter Passion, and three *Hail Marys* in
honor of our Lady of Dolors, to place
yourself under her protection.

Day 1

Jesus Christ Takes Leave of His Blessed Mother

Meditation

During the whole course of His life, Jesus had in an especial manner respected and obeyed His blessed Mother, and had never in the slightest degree been wanting in filial duty; it is, therefore, natural to suppose that, He should give a last proof of His love, by taking leave of so tender a Mother.

1. Consider the indescribable sorrow experienced by Jesus and Mary at the mournful moment of separation.

Jesus, the most affectionate of the sons of men, takes a last farewell of His beloved Mother, before parting from her to go, not to live in a distant land, but to die amidst unspeakable sufferings. What bitter sorrow do they both experience! Mary knows that she is soon to behold her Son agonizing on a Cross, His sacred Body mangled, bleeding, and covered with wounds. O how her maternal heart throbs with anguish! "My beloved Mother," saith Jesus to her, "thou must submit to my delivering Myself up unto death. Such is the will of My Father;

and the redemption of mankind can be
accomplished only at the expense of every drop of
the Blood of Thy Son." At these painful tidings,
what tongue can describe the martyrdom suffered
by the Virginal heart of Mary! She would fain have
made some answer to these words of her beloved
Son, but the intensity of her grief deprives her of the
power. Jesus sighs, and the sorrow He inflicts on
Mary's heart is a source of the deepest anguish to
His own. Mary laments, and the necessity of parting
from Jesus is the sword that inflicts the deepest
wound on her soul. David wept at being separated
from his beloved friend Jonathan, and oh, what tears
of bitter anguish and lively sorrow must Mary have
shed on embracing for the last time her only and
innocent Son about to deliver Himself up to death!
What affliction must Jesus have felt on parting from,
and bidding a last farewell to, the tenderest of
Mothers! O Sacred Hearts of Jesus and Mary! I dare
not ask to fathom the depth of your sorrow at this
separation, but I presume to implore grace to
compassionate and love you, and to weep over my
sins by which I have so many times expelled Jesus

from my heart, renounced His love, and rejected His graces.

2. Consider the generous offering which Mary makes of her Son to suffer death, and of herself to participate in His sufferings:

Mary is a mother, and the heart of a mother cannot naturally nerve itself to dismiss a son to death amidst a thousand tortures for the salvation of guilty man. But the heart of Mary is a generous heart—a heart ready to make the most painful sacrifices for the love of God, and for the benefit of us, her children. She feels her soul pierced through with a sharp sword of grief at being under the necessity of consenting that her beloved Son should deliver Himself up to death. She sees that in losing Jesus she loses a Son who is at once her Father, her God, her All. She comprehends how deep is the sea of sorrow into which her maternal heart is to be plunged at the sight of the innumerable wounds and the barbarous death which await her Son, and of which she is to be a mournful witness. And yet Mary, filled with love for me, and a desire for my salvation, and burning with charity toward God, who requires this painful sacrifice from her, rises superior to herself, offers generously to suffer everything; and although the Passion and Death of Jesus will be to her a source of infinite grief, she willingly, and with her whole heart, gives her consent, and, with more than a martyr's strength of mind, makes the sacrifice of her beloved Son. "Go, my Son!" she says, "Go, to suffer on the Cross; go, even to death; such is the will of Thy Heavenly Father; and such, also, is mine. Would only that I were permitted to die with Thee!"

What charity is displayed toward me by this tender Mother in her submission to the loss of her innocent Son, that I may be saved from eternal death! What strength of mind does she show in willingly offering to endure the most painful martyrdom that I may be saved! Oh, how greatly am I indebted to thy love, my dear Mother! But, oh, how widely does my conduct differ from thine, as regards the acceptation of sufferings, and the sacrifice of anything for the love of my God and for the eternal salvation of my soul! I know well that to be a Christian and a follower of Jesus implies an obligation to suffer. I know that unless I make an offering of my heart and of my affections I shall not save my soul; and yet there is nothing I am more anxious to avoid than the occasions of suffering with Jesus, and of sacrificing my corrupt inclinations for the love of them. O, my dear Mother, obtain for me a share in the strength and generosity of thy most holy heart on all those occasions when I may have to do or suffer anything to please God, and to obtain eternal happiness.

3. Consider the resignation of Jesus and Mary to the Divine will:

When a son is about to die, the mournful news is communicated to the mother by her friends and relations; but here, the Son who is about to endure death—the death of the Cross—Himself makes the painful fact known to Mary, and requires, moreover, that Mary herself should give consent and permission. Maternal affection suggests that she should dissuade Jesus from taking such a step, but resignation to the will of the Eternal Father prevails in her suffering heart, and causes her to exclaim, with heroic submission, though tears are flowing fast from her eyes, "I submit to the Divine will; I consent that Jesus should suffer death." Mary consents to be deprived of her beloved Son, and to pass the remainder of her days overwhelmed with affliction, because it is the will of God that she should cooperate, by her tears, and by the pangs of her sorrowing heart, in the great work of our redemption. When shall we also learn to sacrifice everything to the will of God?

Jesus now leaves Mary, and departs to deliver Himself up to His bitter Passion and ignominious Death. But He goes willingly; because it is the will of His Father that he should suffer and die for our salvation. Oh, how great is the love of Jesus for me! and in what manner do I resign myself to the Divine will for the love of Jesus? How many are my complaints, and how frequent my bursts of impatience, in being forced to submit and resign myself to the dispositions of Providence? Mary parts from the dearest object of her affections—her beloved Son—with the most heroic resignations, and you have not yet detached your heart from the world! You are desirous, perhaps, of taking leave of it, as Jesus did of Mary; but there is no similarity between your position and His, and the world will continue forever answering that you must delay a little longer and enjoy a few more of its pleasures. If you once seek to come to terms with the world, you will never detach yourself from it. God calls you to Himself. God makes known to you His will. It is not His will that you should love the world, but that you should detach yourself from it; make, then a firm resolution to do so, and—in imitation of Jesus and Mary—hasten to execute the will of God.

THE FRUIT

Compassionate Jesus and Mary in their painful trials. Weep over your sins, which were the cause of so much sorrow to their sacred Hearts! Imitate the generous sacrifice of Mary by sacrificing your whole self to Jesus—ready to suffer whatever He may require of you, for love of Him and in expiation of your sins. In every trial be conformed to the will of God, like Jesus and Mary—often exclaiming to Our Lord, in submission and humility of heart, *Fiat voluntas tua!*—Thy will be done!

EXAMPLE

The lovers of Jesus Christ Crucified manifest their devotion and reverence for Him by tenderly kissing the Crucifix, willingly hearing discourses on His sufferings, and attentively reading about them.

Sister Mary Minima, of Jesus of Nazareth, a Carmelite nun, who died in the odor of sanctity, at Vetralla, about the year 1831, was accustomed, while yet a child, frequently to spend some little time in reading accounts of the Passion of Jesus Christ; and so great, even then, was her compassion for her suffering Lord, that she would shed tears in abundance over what she read. After she became a nun, she could not even look at a book upon the Passion, or at any picture or image of Jesus Crucified, without being touched to the heart, and bursting into a flood of tears. She would most tenderly kiss the Crucifix, and was in the habit of spending much time with great compunction of heart in beholding and embracing her Redeemer nailed to the Cross. (See her *Life*). I exhort you also to begin and imitate her, and perform similar devout practices in honor of Christ Crucified, and by degrees you will find your love and devotion towards them sensibly increase.

DAY 2

Jesus is Sold by Judas Iscariot

MEDITATION

Judas having resolved to execute the unholy scheme which he had long been forming in his heart, of betraying his Master, goes secretly to the high priests and elders of the people, and makes them the impious proposal of selling Jesus, and of delivering Him up into their hands.

1. Consider who the man is who sells Jesus.

Not a stranger, not disliked by, nor an enemy of Our blessed Lord. No, one of His disciples, one of the dearest objects of His love, one of His intimate friends, one of the select band most favored by the Divine Master! How can we, in any degree, comprehend the deep grief, the bitter sorrow, experienced by Jesus at such a return from Judas, whom He has always treated with such love and mild forbearance, and on whom He has unsparingly bestowed the most signal favors? Ah, most bitterly does He deplore this enormous crime, of which He has perfect foreknowledge! "Oh!" says Our Lord, in

His Heart, "I am not grieved that a cruel Caiaphas should wish my death; I feel no resentment at being persecuted by an excited and infuriated mob; that a council of the iniquitous scribes and Pharisees is plotting against My life, this does not grieve Me so much; that a heathen judge should unjustly pronounce upon Me the sentence of death on the Cross, this I suffer in peace; but how can I endure that thou—My disciple, My companion, one of My household, and eating at My own table, My intimate friend and apostle, thirsting for My blood—shouldst betray Me and sell Me? Ah, this is too deep a wound for My heart!"

But do you correspond any better with the goodness and love of God when you commit sin? Has He less cause to complain of your ingratitude? Remember all the singular favors which Our Lord has bestowed upon you. He has called you to be His disciple and follower, so that you have had an especial share in His confidence, and in the benefits which He has showered down upon the world. He has bestowed upon you the tender care of a Father. He has admitted you many times to His table, and fed you with His own most precious Body and

Blood. He has loaded you with gifts and graces, besides having prepared for you a kingdom of everlasting beatitude, and you most perfidiously and ungratefully have by sin betrayed your Benefactor, renounced His friendship, bartered away the precious treasure of His grace, and given infinite pain to His loving Heart. Judas sold his Master once only, but can you even remember how many times you have been guilty of the same dark treason? Ah, at least detest your wickedness and, prostrate at the feet of Jesus, weep over the enormity of your crimes, and return, by sincere repentance, to regain your place in His tender Heart, which is still burning with love for you.

2. To whom is Jesus Christ sold by Judas?

The perfidious disciple, to increase the suffering which his Divine Master will experience from the frightful treason he is about to accomplish against His sacred Person, goes to the high priests and heads of the Synagogue, to arrange the terms of the betrayal. And what description of men are these, O Lord, into whose hands one of Thy disciples is meditating and scheming to deliver Thee? They are Thy most cruel enemies, inflamed with rage and hatred against Thee. They have many times sought Thy life. They will rejoice and triumph at having Thee in their power; and they will subject Thee to the most ignominious treatment. This is what in effect came to pass, O my soul, but in the meantime, as Jesus sees and knows all things, how deep is the affliction with which His Heart is overwhelmed at beholding so atrocious an insult offered to His Divine Majesty by one of His Apostles, now an apostate and betrayer of his Lord! And moreover, how must His loving Heart grieve at beholding you so entirely under the dominion of your passions, as to be occupied, day after day, only in finding out new means of satisfying them, and in thinking of committing sin, deserting Jesus, and delivering up your soul into the hands of the devil! Jesus bewailed the perfidy of Judas, but far more does He bewail yours, because it has been so often repeated, and repeated in defiance of so many interior inspirations, of so much remorse of conscience, of so many internal lights, which have reminded and made known to you at how dear a rate Jesus has purchased that soul which you sell to His infernal enemy when you fall into sin. O my Jesus! O my sweet Saviour! I acknowledge and confess my excessive malice. I detest and deplore my past infidelities. Thou didst give me this soul; endow it with Thy grace, sanctify it by Thy Blood, enrich it by Thy merits, and save it from Hell by Thy death; and I, ungrateful for all Thy love, have torn it from Thy arms to sell over and over again to the devil! I implore and beseech Thee to receive my repentant soul which now returns to Thee, and grant, that since it is Thine by right of conquest, it may be Thine for all eternity, and never more have the misfortune to be separated from Thee.

3. The reason for which Judas sells Jesus.

Has any man urged or besought the wicked Apostle to become a traitor, and sell his Divine Master? Has anyone suggested the shameful thought? No. He himself, of his own free will, has offered his services. Oh, how great is the malice and depravity of the human heart! Has he been induced to commit this foul deed through a motive of jealousy or desire of revenge? But how could this have been, since his good Master has neglected no means of gaining his affections, and deterring him from the execution of his design? Again, how could this have been the case, when Jesus, not satisfied with having received him among His disciples, and raised him to the dignity of an Apostle, had bestowed upon him particular marks of love and singular favors? What wrong, or what ill-treatment, can he have received from his adorable Master to stimulate him to take such atrocious vengeance? None whatever. He betrays Him for the sole purpose of satisfying a most depraved passion, which has long tyrannized over his heart, and made him callous and insensible to inspirations, graces, and remorse of conscience. He betrays Him for the sake of a paltry gain, for the sake of obtaining a few pieces of money, with which to gratify his avarice. "What will you give me," says the traitor to the high priests, "and I will deliver my Master to you?" Such is the language held by Judas, as though he were speaking of selling the commonest merchandise! What a degradation for the Person of the Son of God to be thus offered by one of His disciples at the low valuation which His enemies shall please to put upon Him! How painful to His Heart, to behold His precious life sacrificed to the brutal passions of His disciple! The scribes rejoice that one favored by

Christ should offer to be His betrayer, and promise the perfidious wretch thirty pieces of silver as the price of his iniquity. Judas, being quite satisfied with his sacrilegious bargain, closes it at once, and thinks of nothing further than the execution of his agreement. See here into what excesses we may be hurried, if we allow even one single passion to take entire possession of our hearts. Judas was a Prince of the Church, and is thus transformed into a son of perdition. He was in the school of Christ, His familiar friend, and had sat at His table, and is changed in one moment into a demon. Who will not fear? Who can feel secure of standing at beholding such a fall?

You regard Judas with horror, and yet feel none at so often renewing his foul treason by your sins. "What will you give me, and I will deliver unto you Christ, and His grace, and His love, and His friendship," is the language of your heart, when for some vile interest, deceitful hope, or forbidden pleasure, you betray Christ, your duty, and your own conscience. O unhappy merchant, you are indeed at once bereft of sense and of faith! Can the possession of anything in this world compensate for the loss of your soul, and of your God? But, oh, what detestable perfidy is yours! to sell your faithful Friend, your priceless Good, for a mere nothing! Now, at least, expiate your sins by tears of true repentance, and fall prostrate at the feet of Jesus, with the determination henceforth to love and esteem Him above every created object.

THE FRUIT

Examine your heart to see whether you really love God with a love of preference, and value His grace above everything besides. Lose no time in purging your heart of all that can in any way be prejudicial to the love of God. Endeavor to overcome that passion to which you are most addicted, and from which so many of your faults derive their source. Frequently during the course of the day renew your act of contrition at the foot of the Crucifix, for the innumerable faults which you have committed, and which have been so many betrayals of Jesus.

EXAMPLE

The man who is devout to the most holy Passion of Jesus Christ is certain to grasp eagerly at every opportunity of inspiring others with a similar devotion. St. Paul of the Cross, a great lover of Jesus Crucified, was accustomed, while yet a child in his father's house, to make frequent little discourses on the Passion of Jesus Christ, to his brothers and sisters, in order deeply to impress upon their minds the remembrance of the sufferings of their Redeemer. He was accustomed, on these occasions, to take them into his own room, and very devoutly read to them some book on the subject, that so they might be early inspired with sentiments of devotion toward those mysteries which are the fountains of grace. He used to exhort them in the most persuasive terms to reflect often on the sufferings and death of Jesus Christ; and when he left home to found that Order to which he gave the name of *The Passion*, [the Passionist Order] and to preach Jesus Crucified to the people, in which holy employment he passed his whole life, he left them as a legacy these important words: "Constantly bear in mind the sufferings of our Crucified Love." Let these, his last words, be also impressed on your heart. (See his *Life*).

DAY 3

Prayer of Jesus in the Garden

MEDITATION

The Last Supper being over, the discourse finished, and the hymn of thanksgiving said, Jesus leaves the supper-room with His eleven Apostles, and enters the Garden of Gethsemani. Consider—

1. Jesus is in the habit of retiring after the fatigues of the day, to pass the night in solitude and prayer; and even on this last evening of His life He does not depart from His pious custom. Learn hence the great importance of prayer and never neglect it, particularly in spiritual sufferings and trials. Jesus Christ knows that it is in the Garden His Passion is to commence; that in a short time His betrayer is to appear with a body of armed men to arrest Him. He foresees that in a few hours He will have to return by the same road, bound with cords, and dragged along by His enemies, and yet He does not flinch. His ardent charity leads Him onward, and urges Him to enter the Garden without delay, and begin at once to pray and to suffer. Be confounded at the

sight of such an example. The slightest trouble, or the most unimportant business, distracts you from prayer, and the consequences of neglecting to strengthen your soul with that Heavenly food is, that you become weak and languid, sink down, and fall into sin. Ah, my sweet Jesus, through the merits of Thy Passion bestow upon me a spirit of prayer like unto Thine!

2. Jesus prays with the most profound humility. He falls prostrate on the ground before the Majesty of His Divine Father, almost as though He were unworthy to raise His face and eyes to Heaven; and yet He is the Son of God! With what humility should you pray, you, who are but a wretched sinner. Jesus prays with the utmost fervor of spirit, accompanying His prayer with tears, groans, and sighs. In our name, He asks for the graces which we require to save our souls, appeases Divine Justice, and implores pardon for our sins. Cold and languid prayers, such as yours, are not pleasing to God. Jesus prayers in the most lively and tender spirit of confidence, and invokes His Eternal Father, calling Him many times *My Father*. God is our Father, and He loves us like a Father. Can any thought be more

efficacious to excite the firmest sentiments of hope in
our hearts when we pray to this most loving Father?
Jesus prays with the most perfect conformity to the
Divine will. He recommends this afflicted human
nature to His Father; He represents to Him all His
sorrow and sufferings, to excite His compassion; He
implores to be dispensed from drinking the bitter
chalice of His Passion, and yet He prays that what
His Father pleases may come to pass—that the will
of His Father, and not His own, may be done. Learn
to pray in the language and spirit of Jesus Christ,
and to will nothing but what God wills. Finally,
Jesus prays with perseverance, continuing in prayer
for the space of several hours. His most holy soul is
overwhelmed with mortal anguish, and yet He is
neither disturbed nor impatient, but perseveres
constantly in prayer. You may here discover the real
secret of obtaining consolation in affliction; to have
recourse to God, the true Comforter, and never to
grow weary in prayer.

3. After our loving Jesus has three times, with
uplifted eyes, besought His Divine Father that if the
salvation of the world can be accomplished without
His delivering Himself up to death, He may be

dispensed from it, finding that His prayer is not to
be granted, but that, on the contrary, the hour of His
bitter Passion and ignominious death is near at
hand, He permits His suffering humanity to
tremble, and to shudder, and to be overwhelmed
with fear and anguish. Behold how our sorrowing
Jesus, pale, trembling, and anguish-stricken, now
groans, sighs, and seeks to give vent to the profound
internal sorrow oppressing His heart. Oh, how great
is the charity of Jesus! When suffering for me is in
question, His eager love anticipates all the torments
of His Passion. At least compassionate your
Redeemer in this His mortal anguish and make an
offering of yourself to suffer something for love of
Him. Our most afflicted Lord turns in His agony to
His Apostles, to obtain from them some consolation
in His sorrow, and He finds them sleeping. Once
again He has recourse to His Eternal Father, and
receives an inward intimation that it is His will that
He should die for the salvation of men. Jesus bows
down His sacred head, accepts death, and exclaims
with perfect resignation, "Father, Thy will be done!"
Behold at how dear a rate your salvation is
purchased by Jesus! Can you any more grieve at

having to suffer something to save your soul, after all that Jesus has endured for you?

THE FRUIT

Never neglect your accustomed prayer, and when prevented from making it, supply the deficiency by desires, and by frequent aspirations to Jesus suffering. Let your prayer rest solely on the merits of Jesus Christ, unite it with His prayer in the Garden, and offer it up in a true spirit of humility and confidence. Let the prayer *Fiat voluntas tua, Thy will be done*, become familiar to you. In dejection of spirit, in sorrow of heart, and in all your sufferings, remember the internal anguish and affliction endured by Jesus in His prayer in the Garden, and they will be rendered sweet to you.

EXAMPLE

A true lover is always anxious to keep up in his mind a remembrance of the object of his affections, hence souls enamored of Jesus have ever discovered a thousand ingenious ways of keeping alive in their hearts the remembrance of His sufferings. St. Philip Neri always kept near him a figure of Jesus, unfastened from the cross, in order that he might be able the more freely to give vent to the affections of his heart. At night he would place it by his bedside, so that the moment he awoke, he might concentrate all his thoughts upon the sweet Object of his love (see his *Life*). St. Paul of the Cross, when alone in his room always had a very devotional image of Jesus Crucified by his side, and when he went out, he wore it on his breast, so that the sufferings of his Redeemer might be constantly in his thoughts; and in order that so sweet a remembrance might never be effaced from his mind, he wore on his breast, next to the skin, a wooden cross garnished with 186 sharp iron points, which continually pricked him, and thus recalled to his memory the sufferings of Jesus Crucified, and excited his heart to lively feelings of compassion.

DAY 4

The Agony and Bloody Sweat of Jesus in the Garden of Olives

MEDITATION

1. Scarcely has the Angel who appeared from Heaven to comfort Jesus presented Him with the bitter chalice of His Passion, when, by His own will, death displays itself to His mind under the most frightful form, to overwhelm Him with terror. He beholds how in a brief space of time He will be bound like a criminal, scourged as a malefactor, and crucified as a notorious thief. He is fully aware of the inestimable value of His Life, and yet He sees that He must abandon that life to the mercy of His enemies, and lose it by the ignominious death of the Cross. He sees that He is going to die for sins not His own, and the knowledge of His unspotted innocence renders His horror of death more painful still, so that truly no sorrow is like unto His sorrow. But the most painful wound of His tender Heart is inflicted by the thought that there is no one to pity Him. Jesus is about to suffer and die because it is

His own will, and on that very account He suffers more in His agony, because it is at His own command that such painful apprehensions assail Him. Oh, if you could but enter into the Heart of Jesus, how you would now behold Him overwhelmed beneath so indescribable a load of sorrow, as to be in fact reduced to the painful position of the agonizing. Learn now, O my soul, how dear thou art to Jesus. Thy salvation is dearer to Him than His own life. He consents to lose His most precious life to save thine. What then ought to be thy love and gratitude to Jesus?

2. Jesus having excited in Himself the liveliest apprehensions of His approaching death, allows His heart to be oppressed with fear, terror, and horror. Nature would willingly avoid so much suffering, but reason would rather obey God, and accept the chalice of suffering and death, and it is during the course of this painful struggle that Jesus, making a violent effort to vanquish the repugnance of nature, grows pale, faints, and sweats large drops of blood from every part of His sacred Body.

Behold, O my soul, behold thy Redeemer sinking to the earth, overpowered with inward anguish, and bathed in His own Blood! At such a sight, what are thy sentiments? This Blood is not forced from His veins by the fury of His enemies, but wrung from His Heart at His own express desire, that so we may understand the excess of His love for us. Have thy struggles with thy natural inclinations, restraint of thy passions, and submission to the holy will of God, ever cost thee a drop of blood? But the acceptance of death for thy salvation costs Jesus a bloody sweat!

3. Jesus sweats blood to prove how excessive is His hatred for sin. He beholds Himself laden with the sins of the whole world, and His heart is thereby filled with unspeakable horror, so that blood issues from every pore, as though He would wish to shed even tears of blood over our sins! Oh, how great an evil must sin be, since the Son of God enters into an agony, and sweats blood on account of it. How wretched am I if these streams of blood, drawn forth by such excessive love, do not soften my heart! Jesus sweats blood to prove how great is His sorrow for the loss of so many souls infinitely dear to Him, for which He is about to die, and which nevertheless He foresees will be lost through their sins. Ah, who can

understand the anguish of His tender Heart at this thought! Finally, Jesus sweats blood to prove how tenderly He compassionates the elect, and particularly His most holy Mother, in their afflictions and sufferings. Oh, how tender is the love of Jesus, for it seems as though the sufferings of His beloved ones, are more painful to Him than His own! Then, if you have anything to suffer for the love of Jesus, remember that in Him you have a Father who knows how to compassionate, and a God who knows how to reward you.

THE FRUIT

Examine and see what will be your sentiments in your last agony, and live so that the remembrance of your past life may then be a source of consolation to you. In imitation of Jesus, refuse nature everything that is contrary to the will of God. Do violence to yourself if you wish to be saved. Such efforts for the salvation of your soul will not cost you blood, and even if they do, remember that it has cost Jesus yet more. Frequently make an offering to the Eternal Father of the Blood of His Beloved Son in satisfaction for your sins.

EXAMPLE

It is impossible to love Jesus suffering, and not desire to suffer for His sake. St. Philip Neri being moved by meditation on the sufferings of Jesus, and inflamed with love for Him, earnestly desired to go to the Indies and shed his blood for love of Christ, and being unable to follow up his wish, he besought Our Lord to grant that whenever blood should flow from his nose or mouth, it might flow in such abundance as in a degree to correspond with the blood shed by Jesus for the love of him. It was the will of God in some measure to grant his request, for one day he lost so much blood that his eyesight failed, and he fell fainting on the ground (see his *Life*). If you cannot make an offering to Jesus of your blood, you can at least sacrifice to Him one of your passions.

DAY 5

Jesus is Betrayed with a Kiss by Judas

MEDITATION

1. Our Blessed Jesus, after the bloody sweat, by which He was greatly exhausted, rises from prayer, and with admirable courage advances to meet Judas, who at the head of a band of armed men is already approaching the Garden, to betray his Master, and deliver Him up into the hands of His cruel enemies: "Arise," He says to His disciples, "let us go; behold the traitor is at hand. There is no time for sleeping." My soul, what is the source of this courage in Jesus? Prayer. Prayer it is that has filled His soul with heavenly fortitude, and imbued Him with strength to triumph over every difficulty in the obeying of His Father's will. Behold the example which you have to follow. Do you feel any repugnance in overcoming yourself? Do you fear suffering? Do you tremble at the thought of penance? Have recourse to prayer, and then say to your timid shrinking heart, "Arise, let us go to combat our enemies. Let us mortify this passion, let

us pardon that injury. Jesus resisted even unto blood in overcoming His difficulties, it is right that we should follow His example." The more constant you are in the practice of virtue, the more easily will you resist temptation, and very speedily all your sadness and sorrow of heart will be dispelled, if you fortify your soul by prayer.

2. Judas had said to the soldiers, "*Whomsoever I shall kiss, that is He, hold him fast.*" Conformably to his agreement, the traitor draws nigh to Jesus, for the purpose of embracing Him, salutes Him, throws his arms around His neck, calls Him Master, and imprints a kiss upon His sacred face. My soul, give one glance at Judas. Of how many crimes is he not guilty in this single kiss! What execrable perfidy, to make use of the sweetest mark of peace and friendship as a signal of betrayal! What hatred of the blackest die! affectionately to salute Jesus at the very instant of delivering Him up into the hands of His enemies! How atrocious an insult! To call Him *Master* for whose blood and for whose death he is thirsting! Good God! By what means can Judas have fallen so low? Judas the Apostle, the familiar friend of Christ, the witness of His miracles, His disciple,

His companion at the same board! Ah, into what excesses may not, and does not a ruling passion lead us! It blinds our eyes, hardens our hearts, perverts our reason, and finally conducts us even to the depth of iniquity. If you do not early restrain your passions, you will surely fall very speedily into the most fearful crimes.

3. There is no trial more painful to a feeling heart than to be betrayed, and there never has been more frightful treachery than that of Judas, and yet observe with what meekness and patience Jesus submits to what is a source of such acute sorrow to His tender Heart. He repels not that unnatural monster of ingratitude, but receives him with humility and sweetness, and embraces him with every demonstration of the most ardent charity. He selects this last moment to bestow upon His betrayer the tenderest additional proofs of unbounded love, and by the interior movements of His grace and exterior demonstrations of friendship, He calls, invites, and urges him to repent and be converted. Oh, charity of my Jesus! When will you also learn not to resent an offense, and not to be so unforgiving toward those who offend you? When will you learn

from the example of Jesus to bear patiently any trifling injury?

Jesus answers the traitor who is making such an assault upon His sacred Person, calls him His *friend*, assures him of His love by His encouraging language, and offers him His pardon and friendship. "*Friend*," He says, with ineffable sweetness, "*whereto art thou come? Dost thou betray the Son of Man with a kiss?*" But Judas is as a deaf man, and persists in his crime. How many times, when you have been on the point of committing sin, has Jesus most lovingly called you by name, and said to your heart, "*Son dost thou betray Me thus? What harm have I done thee that thou shouldst thus offend Me?*" But you were as a deaf man, and continued in sin. Weep over your ingratitude, and return to Jesus.

THE FRUIT

Do not flatter yourself that you love God, if you allow any passion to predominate in your soul. Examine this day what your predominate passion is; resolve to overcome it at any cost, and to resist all its unjust pretensions. Ask God's pardon for the ingratitude with which you have frequently corresponded so ill with His loving inspirations, and in time of temptation; or when in danger of committing sin, imagine that you hear Jesus saying to you, *"Wilt thou betray Me thus?"* and you will never have heart to offend so good a Father.

EXAMPLE

In the midst of your occupations, and even of your amusements, you may keep up in your heart a lively remembrance of the sufferings of Jesus Christ. St. Philip Neri frequently used to take several youths to an open spot, where they could recreate their minds with some innocent amusements, which he himself would set on foot; and then he would retire aside to read or meditate on some point of the Passion out of a little book which contained the whole history, and which he accustomed to carry about with him. (See his *Life*). What is there to prevent you also from retiring at least in the recesses of your heart from time to time, to bestow one look of love and compassion upon your suffering Jesus?

DAY 6

Jesus is Taken and Bound by the Soldiers

MEDITATION

1. The Jews would never have succeeded in taking and binding Jesus, if He had not so willed; and having fallen to the ground at the mere sound of His voice, they never could have risen again, if Jesus had not first given them permission. But the love of Jesus cannot endure that the Passion, which He has so earnestly desired, should be longer deferred. His enemies are burning with impatience to lay hands upon His sacred Person, and bear Him away a prisoner, and equally does Jesus burn with impatience to be deprived of liberty and life for love of us. Oh, how great is the charity of Jesus! If I really loved Jesus, I should not so carefully avoid even the shadow of suffering for His sake, while He goes forth eagerly to endure torments and death for mine. Jesus might fly, or escape in some other way out of the hands of His enemies, or He might command the assistance of many legions of angels. But He does nothing of the sort, because He desires

to die. He allows Himself to be taken and bound, and it is for this very purpose that He goes forth to meet His enemies, and draws nigh to them with a sweet, mild, and loving countenance, like a victim that is led to sacrifice for the salvation of mankind. Jesus allows Himself to be bound, because His bonds are to break the chains of our sins. Jesus becomes a slave for our sakes, through the excess of His charity alone, to free our souls from the slavery of the devil. Offer yourself to Him now, to be entirely His, beseeching Him to bind you fast with the sweet chains of His love.

2. While Jesus Christ, with tranquil heart and serene countenance, permits Himself to be taken by His enemies, they, on their side, fall upon Him with diabolical fury, and bind Him fast lest He should again escape them, whilst each man rejoices and triumphs at the grand capture that has been made. Full of rage and hatred, they smite Him with their hands, throw Him on the ground, strike Him with their feet, drag Him along with violence, and ill-treat His sacred Person in every possible way. What but love for you has reduced Jesus to so lamentable a condition? There is none to defend, none to

console Him. All His disciples have deserted Him.
And yet all protested but a few hours previously
that they would die with Him.

How many times have you also protested that
you would follow and imitate Jesus, and yet, when
occasion has offered, you have abandoned Him! O
thoughtlessness of an ungrateful soul! Jesus makes
no resistance to His cruel enemies; Jesus shows no
resentment; but, on the contrary, with a heart
burning with love for His Heavenly Father, He
rejoices that the long sighed-for hour of suffering is
come at last, and that He is to make satisfaction for
our sins by His Passion and Death. When will you
learn from the example of Jesus to submit patiently
to affronts and injuries?

3. Indescribable is the barbarity manifested by
the furious enemies of Jesus Christ in their treatment
of His sacred Person, but equally wonderful is His
unalterable patience. They bind His neck, hands,
and waist together, with cords and chains, as though
He were the most wicked of malefactors, and Jesus
refuses not to wear these chains, but accepts them
with joy and offers them up to His Eternal Father,
thereby to merit for us the liberty of the children of

God. Contemplate Jesus in the hands of sinners, loaded with chains, and bound with cords; enter in thought with all possible reverence into His sacred Heart, and see how He suffers not so much from those chains and cords as from the sight of the sins of the whole world, with which He is loaded, and which form a chain so oppressive and painful as to overwhelm and bow Him down to the ground. Yet He submits to its weight with the most heroic fortitude through His earnest desire of breaking it asunder, and liberating our souls. O infinite mercy of my Jesus! Thou art intent solely upon delivering and saving me, while I, instead of compassionating Thee thus bound, and breaking asunder those chains which torture and oppress Thee, increase their weight by adding to the number of my sins. I beseech Thee, my sweet Jesus, that now, once for all, I may put a stop to such malice. May I now at least begin to return Thee love for love.

THE FRUIT

Jesus, when ill-treated, beaten, and bound, is silent and complains not; learn from his example to restrain your feelings, to bridle your tongue, and to accept in peace and bear with meekness whatever may befall you that is trying to self-love. Carefully examine whether you are enslaved to any bad habit or evil passion, promise Jesus that you will at any cost burst all such hateful bands, and beseech Him to bind your soul closely to Himself by the chains of holy love.

EXAMPLE

The remembrance of the sufferings of Jesus renders all pains and sorrows sweet and light. A friend of St. Paul of the Cross being astonished at his austere and penitential mode of life, and unable to understand how so weak and sickly a man could endure such continual, excessive sufferings, questioned him one day on the subject. "Tell me, Father Paul," he said, "how you contrive to lead such a life?" The servant of God replied with deep emotion, "Jesus Christ has suffered so much for love of me, it is not therefore wonderful that I should do and suffer something for love of Him." (See his *Life*). When you feel any repugnance to suffering, say the same to yourself, and you will soon feel the beneficial effects of such a reflection.

Day 7

Jesus is led before the Tribunal of Annas

Meditation

1. Jesus being taken and bound by the Jews, is violently dragged from the Garden to Jerusalem, to be presented before the tribunal of Annas, the High Priest. Never has any culprit, or even any notorious malefactor, been treated with such barbarous cruelty as is the most innocent Son of God upon this occasion. One man drags Him forward, another smites, another insults, another blasphemes, another maltreats His sacred Person in diverse ways. And what is the demeanor of Jesus under such an accumulation of outrages and sufferings? Without uttering one word of complaint, without making the slightest demonstration of anger, or desire of revenge, He advances like a meek lamb led to the slaughter. Jesus, with one single word, might have struck terror into His enemies, and yet He submits to everything in patient silence. He might in one moment have delivered Himself from their fury, and yet willingly subjects Himself to it, and regards all

their insults and outrages as so many outbursts of the anger of God punishing the sins of the world in His sacred humanity, and He implores mercy for us, offering them all to His Eternal Father. Behold our blessed Jesus walking in the midst of this insolent band of soldiers, His head bowed down, His eyes bent on the ground, His hands bound, His face disfigured with blows, His whole frame exhausted and trembling, and with scarcely the strength to proceed further. Can it be possible that a Christian with such a spectacle before his eyes, should continue to be proud, should give way to anger, should be unable to preserve a moment's silence under affronts, or be unwilling to bear the slightest injury. Ah, shame, shame upon your own self, for you have truly deserved all the outrages and affronts which are heaped upon your innocent Jesus!

2. As soon as the Jews arrive at Jerusalem, they conduct Jesus to the house of Annas, enter the great hall without delay, and present the Holy of Holies before the High Priest, as a malefactor. Jesus remains standing, bound like a criminal, before His proud judge, who examines Him concerning His disciples and His doctrine. What a sight to behold! The Son of

God, the Eternal High Priest, the universal Judge of all mankind, presented before an earthly tribunal to be judged by a sinful, proud, hypocritical man! What must the Angels have thought on beholding their Lord in a state of such deep humiliation? But what do you say to so wonderful an example of humility and patience, you who seek applause and the esteem of men—you who cannot endure to see an equal preferred before you—you who so greatly fear the judgments of men, and who, although but a sinner, yet shrink from being thought such? Observe your most patient Jesus standing before the tribunal of Annas, and with what serenity of countenance, intrepidity of heart, and modesty of speech, He who is innocence itself, submits to be judged by a sinner. Oh, what will be your fate when you shall appear before Jesus Christ, your judge, and be convicted of having so little profited by His example, and of having led a life directly in opposition to His teaching?

3. Consider how painful it must be to Jesus to behold His character defamed, while His disciples utter not a word in His defense. He looks round to see whether there are any of His friends or followers

to interest themselves in His behalf, but there is not one man to come forward in His defense. Every day do not you also inflict this wound anew upon His Divine Heart, when you remain cold and insensible, and take no pains to defend the honor of God attacked by sinners, or the sanctity of religion blasphemed by the impious. Our most afflicted Redeemer beholds also brought forward a number of false witnesses, who by their accusations conspire to hasten His condemnation. By the slightest bid of His omnipotence He might have silenced all these wretches, who have been formerly the witnesses of His miracles, or benefited by His loving charity. But Jesus is silent, and endures their execrable ingratitude with indescribable patience. How long has Jesus patiently borne with you, who, after having received so many benefits from His liberal hand, never cease most ungratefully to offend and outrage Him? Ah, my sweet Saviour, grant through Thy great mercy that I may from this moment cease to be ungrateful to Thy love.

THE FRUIT

God is greatly glorified when we humbly accept those mortifications and humiliations which daily fall to our lot. Reflect on what may happen to you in particular, and resolve that such shall be your conduct. Fear not the judgments of men, and far less allow yourself to be persuaded to neglect virtuous actions and works of piety for fear of what the world will say. Love to be considered imperfect, and to appear a sinner before men, but strive with all the energy of your soul not to be such before God.

EXAMPLE

The remembrance of the sufferings of Jesus inspires a man with long enduring patience under injuries. It once happened that St. Paul of the Cross was making a voyage in the same ship with some individuals who, forgetting the sanctity of their character, seasoned their discourse rather freely with indecent expressions. The good Father mildly reproved them, and sought in the most charitable manner to bring them to a sense of their fault, but they, burning with anger against their benefactor, overwhelmed him with such a torrent of abuse and scornful words as to horrify all who listened to them. The humble servant of God, calling to mind the outrages offered to Jesus in His Passion, remained perfectly silent, without being in the slightest degree discomposed, and with the most serene and peaceful expression of countenance. Are you desirous of gaining a similar victory over yourself? Adopt the same means.

DAY 8

Jesus Receives a Blow

MEDITATION

It appeared to the Evangelist that so great a wrong was done to Jesus when He received a blow, that it deserved particular mention as a subject worthy of our meditation. Consider—

1. This insult is of a most degrading character.

Jesus is a King of infinite Majesty, the Eternal Son of God, and yet receives a blow from the hand of a servant. Can any affront bear comparison with this? Jesus receives a blow on His face, in the presence of a large multitude, and of the high priest and heads of the people. Thus, then, is the Majesty of God outraged by a presumptuous slave! The Heavens themselves must have recoiled with horror at such a sight! Jesus receives a blow, which is so great an outrage to His dignity that the mere thought causes you to burn with zeal and indignation against the brutal wretch who gave it: yet Jesus bears it patiently, makes not a gesture of anger, and indulges not in the slightest desire of revenge. You regard an opprobrious word as a dreadful offense, and magnify a slight act of discourtesy into a grievous insult, to which you imagine you cannot possibly submit. Do you call such slight grievances as these equal to the blow received by Jesus? Are you more noble, more worthy of veneration than Jesus? Can it be possible that you are nourishing thoughts of resentment and revenge, when your God endures the ignominy of being struck on the face with such admirable patience?

2. The blow is given most unjustly.

The person who gives it possesses no authority, but, in order to please the high priest, smites Jesus heavily on the face, at the same time reproving Him with arrogant boldness for having offended the judge. How many times have you imitated the example of this wretch? To please such or such a friend, or to satisfy such or such an unworthy passion, have you outraged Jesus. Jesus receives this blow for no reason whatever, solely on account of a pretended fault against the High Priest, as though our most humble Redeemer were bold and insolent in His demeanor. He had spoken, it is true, but with the greatest modesty, prudence, and Divine wisdom, and for this is He punished by a blow. Could there be more manifest injustice? And yet no one reproves the daring servant—no one condemns such an unjust proceeding—no one compassionates our innocent Lord, but on the contrary, all rejoice at this outrage, while Heaven itself is silent, and does not strike dead the man who dares to be guilty of such an atrocity. But far more reason have you to wonder that Heaven and earth have not united to exterminate a being like yourself, who have so many times had the boldness to offend your God and Creator by sin. Can anyone be more daring and insolent than you, who have offended God, notwithstanding all the obligations you are under of loving Him?

3. This blow is given in a cruel manner, and therefore inflicts severe pain upon Jesus Christ.

It is given with all the energy of anger, with all the force of a strong arm, and perhaps even with a hand covered with an iron gauntlet. What pain must our patient Jesus have endured! The sacred face of Jesus is peculiarly delicate and susceptible to pain: what suffering then must a merciless blow on it cause! Behold how the Divine countenance, which ravisheth all hearts, is discolored and bruised by that cruel blow! See how the blood flows from eyes, nostrils, and mouth! Can we look upon that sacred Face thus disfigured, without being moved to compassion? Oh, if we could but behold the interior of the heart of our amiable Saviour at this moment! What burning charity towards him who gave the blow, what tender love towards me, for whose sake He suffers, and desires to suffer still more, should we there behold! How far am I from imitating Thee, O my Jesus! I cannot bear a sharp word, I cannot submit to even a just reproof, and I feel a secret aversion for those whom I ought to love. I beseech Thee to impress upon my mind and heart the remembrance of Thy admirable patience.

THE FRUIT

You are impatient because you are proud. Pride makes you think the slightest wrong done you a real injury, although in fact no wrong can ever be done you, as you deserve, by reason of your sins, far more than you can possibly receive. Let the remembrance of all that Jesus has suffered for them be ever present to your mind, and you will speedily learn humility and patience. Seek for occasions of public humiliation, imposed either by yourself or by others, thus to repair the scandal you have given by your pride.

EXAMPLE

The man who maintains a lively recollection of the sufferings of Jesus Christ, esteems all trials light. St. Paul of the Cross one day entered a church to assist at Benediction of the Blessed Sacrament, when some boys knocked over a heavy bench which fell on his foot, bruising and hurting it exceedingly. The servant of God without displaying any emotion, raised up the bench, kissed it, and then continued his prayer. His companion, observing that blood was flowing from the wounded foot, told the good Father of it, but he still remained perfectly quiet. When they left the church, his companion again begged him to look at his foot and have the wound dressed, but the servant of God replied: "These slight sufferings are roses to me, for Jesus Christ has endured much more, and I deserve infinitely more,

on account of my sins." And he would not even look
at his wound. (See his *Life*).

DAY 9

Jesus before Caiaphas

MEDITATION

Annas being unable to discover any grounds for condemning Jesus Christ, and yet being desirous that He should be condemned, sends Him to the High Priest Caiaphas, and leaves the decision of the case to him. Contemplate Jesus thus taken before a second tribunal.

1. Our Blessed Lord, bound like a thief, is conducted through the public streets of Jerusalem accompanied by a large body of soldiers who indulge their rage and hatred by ill-treating Him in every possible way, and surrounded by a multitude of people who overwhelm Him with insults and maledictions, and rejoice over His misfortunes. Jesus advances, His feet bare, and His strength utterly exhausted by all His mental and bodily sufferings, offering up the ignominy and tortures He is now enduring, to His Eternal Father, for the salvation of my soul. The soldiers render His position still more painful, by inviting people to approach and see their

renowned prisoner, while Jesus proceeds on His way in the midst of them, with a humble demeanor and with downcast eyes, to teach us what value we should set on the esteem and honor of the world, and the applause of men. But a few days previously Jesus had passed through these same streets, applauded and honored by the crowd as the Messias, and now, abandoned even by His disciples, He is followed only by perfidious enemies who seek His death, and unite in deriding and insulting Him as a malefactor, and the last of men. Such is the duration of the honors and praises of the world! Learn hence to seek the good pleasure of God alone, to labor for the acquisition of a right to the immortal honors of Paradise, and to practice patience under humiliation, from the example of Jesus.

2. The Doctors and Ancients of the Synagogue are all assembled in the house of Caiaphas, awaiting the arrival of Christ, and as soon as they perceive Him approaching, they begin to consult together concerning the best way of condemning Him. They are thirsting for His blood, they are eager for His death, but it is not sufficient for their purpose that He should die, He must also die as a criminal, and

with the disgrace of having merited death. Witnesses are summoned from all parts, and liberty is given to every one to accuse the innocent Saviour of the world. The hall of the Great Council is filled with people, and in front of all stands Jesus, as a criminal, with His hands bound, and in an attitude of profound humility and meekness. Every one invents at will accusations, brings forward all that rage and jealousy can dictate, to stain the fair fame of our sweet Jesus, and utter the most atrocious calumnies against Him who is innocence itself. Jesus listens in silence, and His Heart is oppressed with sorrow that such horrible lies should be uttered, nevertheless His patience never wavers, and He prays for His calumniators with the tenderest charity. Jesus holds His peace, not because He is unable to justify Himself, but to teach you by His mysterious silence that whenever your own innocence alone is concerned there is no better weapon than humble silence for the refutation of calumny.

3. Caiaphas seeing that none of the witnesses can bring forward sufficient proof of any of their accusations for Jesus to be condemned, and that He,

notwithstanding every provocation, still remains silent, gives the rein to his fierce passions, and adjures our Saviour, in the name of God, to tell him whether He is the Son of the Most High. Jesus is perfectly conscious that the Jews will make any acknowledgment of His Divinity serve as a specious pretext for condemning Him to death; and yet, so great is His love of truth, and respect for the adorable name of God, that He replies with angelic modesty of demeanor, "*I am.*"

No sooner has the wicked High Priest heard the humble answer of Jesus Christ, than he rends his sacerdotal garment as if through horror of an execrable blasphemy, hypocritically exaggerates the enormity of the supposed crime, and draws from thence the conclusion that Jesus must be condemned to death as a blasphemer. The whole Council concur in this sentence, and tumultuously raising their voices, exclaim: "He is worthy of death!"

Compassionate our suffering Redeemer in this painful situation. He is forced to speak when He prefers silence; and, when at length He utters a word, that word is construed into a crime deserving of death. The detractions and calumnies of the wicked have always threatened the lives of the just, but the just have always found in the example of their Saviour ample consolation for all outrages. Jesus is treated as a blasphemer, and He bears the ineffable wrong done Him with the most patient meekness. If you keep His example before your eyes, you will no longer have any difficulty in supporting the most disgraceful calumnies.

THE FRUIT

It is not sufficient to submit to humiliations and calumnies; you must, moreover, submit to them with the intention of imitating Jesus, and for the love of Him. Make a firm resolution that you will remember the humble and patient demeanor of Jesus Christ amidst the outrages and false accusations of His enemies, in order to encourage yourself to follow His example. Carefully repress your natural inclination to speak in your own defense, and offer up your silence to Jesus.

EXAMPLE

Meditation on the sufferings of Jesus teaches us patience under the most painful trials. Blessed Osanna of Cataro, being one day oppressed with a burning fever, besought the Almighty to grant her some relief, when Jesus Christ appeared to her, covered with wounds and streaming with blood, and said, "Daughter, why dost thou grieve so much over thy sufferings and not rather over the bitter tortures which I have endured for love of thee?" So deep was the impression made upon the mind and heart of the servant of God by the words and appearances of Jesus, that henceforward, far from complaining, she would exclaim, "Oh, what agony has Jesus endured in His Passion! How can we have the heart to complain?" (See her *Life*). Accustom yourself to compare your sufferings with those of Jesus, and you will soon cease to be impatient.

Day 10

Jesus Christ is Denied by Saint Peter

Meditation

Three times did Saint Peter deny his Divine Master; let us therefore, meditate upon the causes of those denials, which were at once so insulting and so painful to our blessed Jesus

1. He denies Jesus through the tepidity of his love for Him.

The love of Peter for his Master had greatly cooled. He had slept when he should have prayed. He had followed Jesus *afar off*, and more through curiosity than affection, *to see the end*. Instead of compassionating his Lord in His Passion, he was listening to idle conversation. In short, idleness, listlessness, curiosity, and neglect of prayer—all fatal marks of tepidity—prepared the soul of Peter for his unhappy fall. A soul cannot remain long in a state of tepidity, without falling into serious faults. The passions grow stronger as the love of God becomes weaker. The devil assaults the soul with a degree of violence increased in proportion to her neglect of prayer. God withdraws His special graces from the tepid soul, to punish her criminal languor. In this state, she is, as it were, on the very edge of a deep, perhaps even, bottomless abyss, and the slightest push is sufficient to cast her down headlong. If you have grown cold in the practice of virtue, negligent in prayer, forgetful of the presence of God, and indulgent in your passions, delay not for a moment to return to your first fervor, otherwise you will end by committing great sins, and perhaps at last incur eternal damnation.

2. Peter denies Jesus through presumption and self-confidence.

It almost always happens that interior sentiments of pride precede the commission of grievous sins. Peter was not aware of his own weakness. He preferred himself before others; he trusted in himself as though he were incapable of sinning, boasting that no temptation would separate him from Jesus. He would not even believe the assurance of his Divine Master, that he would deny Him thrice. Deceived by this vain confidence in his own strength, he neglects to pray, and to have recourse to God; and God, in His justice, permits him to fall, in punishment of his pride. There is nothing more dangerous than to confide in our own strength, and trust to feelings of fervor. We are full of malice, and capable of committing the most enormous crimes, unless God supports us. Who can now yield to temptations of pride? The Saints have fallen. Peter, the most fervent of all the Apostles, falls after having passed three years in the school of Christ, and been taught by His Divine lips, and been so favored by Him, and after having protested so many times that he would rather die than offend Him! Peter denies all knowledge of Him, even with oaths and imprecations. Good God! how low may we fall in one moment! Be on your guard against yourself and your own weakness, and continually implore the help of Divine Grace.

3. Saint Peter denies Jesus, because he rashly exposes himself to the occasions of sin.

He remains in the company of the soldiers—a licentious and dissolute set of men—and becomes on such intimate terms with them as to warm himself at the same fire. Evil company is a most dangerous occasion of sin. If you do not avoid the society of the wicked, you will end by becoming like them. Saint Peter, alarmed at the voice of a servant, denies Jesus, and thus commits one sin; but still he does not avoid the dangerous occasion, or fly from that place and company which have already been fatal to him. Consequently, he sins a second and a third time, and would never have entered into himself, nor risen from the deep abyss into which he had fallen, had not Jesus Christ, by a loving look of mercy enlightened and raised him up. Every time you have fallen into mortal sin, you have denied Jesus. As often as you have exposed yourself to the danger of committing sin, so often have you declared by your actions that you know not Jesus, who has commanded you to fly from the occasions of denying Him. Ah! by the love you bear your own soul, always tremble with horror at the thought of returning to those occasions where you have at other times fallen into sin! Tremble, and fly, if you do not wish to offend God.

THE FRUIT

Saint Peter fell into sin for one brief hour, and bewailed his fall during the whole remainder of his life. Never did he forget that he had sinned and displeased his beloved Master. By how many enormous faults have you displeased your good God, your amiable Redeemer? Repeatedly renew your acts of contrition. Saint Peter did not for one moment delay his repentance and conversion. How long has God called and invited you to repentance? Resolve this very day to be converted to God. Do not wait till tomorrow, as perhaps tomorrow, time for you may be no more.

EXAMPLE

The thought of Jesus suffering is a remedy against all the assaults of the devil. Blessed Christina of Cologne, being tormented by devils, interiorly with horrible temptations, and exteriorly with blows and other tortures, was accustomed to repel their assaults and preserve her soul in patience amidst so many trials, by the remembrance of the sufferings of Jesus. "If I look at Jesus dying on the Cross for my sake," she would say, "I do not fear to endure all that Hell can inflict on me for His love." "When I remember how my innocent Jesus was transfixed by cruel nails," she would exclaim to the demons, "I offer myself willingly to suffer any tortures from your hands, that so I may have a share in His dolorous Passion." The utterance of these few words either freed her from the evil spirits, or enabled her to preserve unalterable serenity of mind. (Bollandists, June 22).

Day 11

Jesus is Derided and Treated Most Ignominiously in the House of Caiaphas

Meditation

The iniquitous sentence having been pronounced by Caiaphas, Jesus remains for the whole concluding portion of that night in the power of His enemies, who keep Him bound in chains, and cruelly maltreat His sacred Person. Consider all that Jesus suffers during this night.

1. He suffers in His sacred Body.

The first outrage offered to the meek Redeemer of the world is that His enemies spit in His face. No greater insult or more decided mark of contempt can be shown to a man of honor than to spit in his face. Not once only is the face of Jesus, the only Son of God, defiled with spittle, but over and over again is He outraged in that manner by the whole band of insolent soldiers and servants, who seem to vie with each other in insulting Him. And in defiling His adorable countenance with their filthiness. What an ignominious outrage, what a shameful degradation, is this for our most patient Jesus! And yet He turns not away His face, but suffers, and is silent. Such are the humiliations caused to Jesus by our vanity! By the endurance of such grievous insults does Jesus expiate my pride! The second torture inflicted on Jesus is that of being struck with the hands and feet of His enemies, who at the same time maltreat Him in various other ways. Contemplate our sweet Saviour thus abandoned to the mercy of these cruel wretches, who joyfully take advantage of this opportunity of satiating their rage by smiting Him with barbarous energy. See how the whole of the sacred Body of our dear Lord is, in the course of a few moments, bruised and disfigured by a shower of heavy blows! Ah, to what sufferings, to what torturing insults, is our blessed Jesus subjected for the love of you, an ungrateful creature! And you remain unmoved by so mournful a spectacle? Do you not compassionate Jesus? Do you not at least desire to imitate His patience, humility, and silence?

2. He suffers in His honor.

The patience and unalterable mildness of Jesus serve but to excite the fury of His enemies, who continue with diabolical perseverance to invent new modes of torturing Him. Not satisfied with the more common insults and scornful expressions with which they have hitherto accompanied their blows, they now treat Him as a false prophet. They cover His face with a filthy rag, and deride Him as though He were a fool or a madman. They blindfold Him, to be able to maltreat His sacred Person more unrestrainedly, and display increased fury and insolence in their outrages. They blaspheme, they smite, they curse Him, without remorse or restraint. Behold to what an excess sinners have carried their outrages against Jesus! But behold also to what an excess Jesus has carried His heroic patience! He is the God of wisdom, the Lord of prophets, and the Searcher of hearts, yet He permits Himself to be dishonored so far as even to be treated as a fool or maniac, and the scorn of men! He might in one moment have taken ample vengeance on those who outrage Him, but it is His Will to teach you by His example not to be so sensitive to all that affects your reputation and honor, to submit to a slight insult for His sake, to overcome human respect, and to make a sacrifice to Him of your anxious desire for honor and esteem.

3. He suffers in His soul.

It is impossible to describe all that Jesus suffers in His most holy Soul during this night of agony. He has a clear knowledge of the heinousness of the insults offered to Him, because He is well aware of the excellence of His Divine Person, thus loaded with contumely; He comprehends that the Majesty of God is therein most shamefully outraged, and that by those very men to whom He had been most untiringly liberal of His favors; hence how deep is the affliction which overwhelms His tender Heart! He hears the obscene language, the curses and calumnies, of those brutal soldiers, and they are so many wounds lacerating His pure Soul. He beholds Himself loaded with ignominy and opprobrium, defiled with spittle, and reduced so as to be a *worm, and no man*. He who is the God of Majesty and Glory, —what confusion, what agony, must have been His! And yet Jesus, even when His interior anguish is at its height, rejoices in submitting to every species of outrage, thus to make satisfaction for my sins, and to apply to my soul the infinite merit of all His sufferings. Admire the boundless charity of Jesus, and never cease thanking Him for all He has vouchsafed to endure for your salvation.

THE FRUIT

When you contemplate the spectacle of the Jews defiling the adorable face of Jesus with spittle, remember that you also have done like them every time that you have offended God by impure and immodest words. Excite yourself to sentiments of contrition for your sins, and make a firm determination to place a guard upon your tongue, and exert the most watchful vigilance. During the day, whenever your patience is tried, contemplate Jesus in the hands of His enemies, who inflict the most disgraceful tortures upon Him, while He utters not one word of complaint.

EXAMPLE

Blessed Serafino of Ascoli, a Capuchin friar, was frequently tried, while yet a young man in the world, by the reproofs and sneers of his companions, and the unjust severity of one of his brothers, who was so cruel as sometimes even to refuse him a dry crust of bread. The pious youth submitted to everything with admirable patience, all his sufferings being rendered sweet to him by the remembrance of those of Christ. Meditation on the Passion of his Lord was his sole consolation amid the numerous trials he had to endure. A like comfort will it be to you, if you follow his example. (See his *Life*).

DAY 12

Jesus is Led before Pilate, the Roman Governor

MEDITATION

Early in the morning, the high priests and ancients of the people again assemble and resolve to deliver Jesus up to the secular power, by consigning Him to Pontius Pilate, a Gentile, and the Governor of Judea, Consider—

1. The exterior of Jesus during this His third most painful journey.

He is bound anew with cords and chains by order of the high priests, that Pilate may at once regard Him as a man guilty of death, and unworthy of being treated with clemency. Thus bound, our sweet Saviour is dragged by the inhuman Jews, who overwhelm Him with every species of insult, as the very worst of malefactors, before the tribunal of the governor. The streets are crowded, and new spectators throng in from every side to feast their eyes upon the prisoner. All rejoice, and all endeavor by bitter insults to share in the torture of the innocent malefactor. And among all this crowd watching and deriding Him, there is scarcely one man to be found who pities Him. My soul, contemplate this Man-God bound with heavy chains, His sacred face discolored and defiled with spittle, His head uncovered and bruised by the blows He has received, and His whole Divine Person outraged at every step by the most degrading insults. Contemplate the modesty and gravity of His demeanor, and behold how His sacred countenance is expressive of the most serene patience and meek humility. Thou canst not perceive there the slightest trace of vexation, sorrow, or anger.

His strength is exhausted, He is sinking with fatigue, and bowed down beneath the ignominy of His situation, yet He hastens onward joyfully and serenely to deliver Himself up into the hands of Pilate, to be condemned to death. Oh, what charity, what mercy, what condescension, is Thine, my Jesus! And all for my sake! But oh, what lessons of virtue may I not draw from thy outward deportment on this occasion!

2. The interior of Jesus.

He is thoroughly aware of all the evil intentions of His enemies, who are resolved to have Him put to death as a public malefactor; therefore we might naturally suppose that He would be thereby afflicted and filled with indignation; but, on the contrary, the calmness of His Heart remains undisturbed, and His appearance is that of a meek Lamb led to the slaughter. He sees that the Jews have unanimously conspired against Him through motives of malice and hatred, that there is not one man to stand by Him, and that all are afraid of speaking in His favor—still, our innocent Redeemer humbles Himself amid all His sufferings, as though He were really guilty. He hears the insulting words, the sharp sarcasms, and the atrocious calumnies with which every one of His enemies delights in assailing Him, and He offers all with fervent acts of charity to His Eternal Father in expiation of my sins. He permits His senses to feel the whole bitterness of His sufferings, but, at the same time, His soul is overflowing with joy that the day for which He has long sighed, and for which he has been waiting during the space of thirty-three years, to accomplish the work of my Redemption, is come at last. Compare your interior dispositions for one moment with those of Jesus. How great a difference do we behold between them! You can bear nothing willingly, like Jesus. You grieve, lament, are disturbed in spirit, and have not even sufficient fortitude to offer your slight trials to Jesus, who has suffered so much for love of you. When will you profit by the example of Jesus?

3. Jesus before Pilate.

The Jews might have put Jesus to death secretly, and thus satiated their feelings of hatred and envy, but they are desirous of appearing innocent of His death: they wish that He should die, but not that the odium of His death should be imputed to them. They therefore conduct Him to Pilate, that he may pronounce the sentence of condemnation, and, without entering into his palace, they loudly call upon him to condemn to death the malefactor whom they have brought loaded with chains before his tribunal. Pilate, from his house, beholds our blessed Jesus advancing toward Him with the utmost meekness and humility of demeanor, and he perceives how He is almost visibly surrounded by a halo of innocence. The Jews well know the perfect innocence of Jesus, and still, with senseless fury, clamorously demand His death. A hundred times have they received proofs of His goodness; over and over again has He been to them a loving benefactor, and now they are seeking only to have Him put to death as the worst of malefactors. Let not your anger be kindled against the Jews, but against yourself, for whenever you have committed sin your crime has been far greater than theirs, in outraging your Benefactor, your Father, and your God. You knew what you were doing; you believed in Jesus, and yet sinned!

Meanwhile, Jesus stands before the governor in humble silence, surrounded by His enemies, and is desirous of giving an example of patience rather than of proving His innocence. Oh, how instructive is His silence!

THE FRUIT

When tempted to commit sin, and to offend Jesus, answer the devil, the world, and your own passions, in the words of Pilate to the Jews when they presented Christ before his tribunal: *"What accusations bring you against this man?* What evil has Jesus done to me that I should offend Him? Has He deserved to be offended? Ought I to hate Him who has so much loved me?" If you direct all your efforts to the acquisition of the interior virtues of meekness, mildness, and humility of heart, you will find no difficulty in the practice of other, exterior virtues.

EXAMPLE

The remembrance of the Passion of Jesus detaches the soul from worldly vanities. St. Elizabeth of Hungary, having entered a church one festival day to assist at the Divine office, dressed in her royal robes, and attended by a large retinue of servants, cast her eyes upon a Crucifix, and at that sight her heart immediately smote her. "Behold thy Creator," said an inward voice, "thy Redeemer, thy God, who for love of thee hangs naked on a Cross, and suffers the most disgraceful of deaths, and thou, a wretched creature, art clothed in vain attire and costly ornaments. The head of Jesus is crowned with thorns, and thine with flowers and jewels. Thus, then, dost thou imitate thy Master, thus dost thou follow His example!" So deeply was she touched and overcome by these reflections that she turned pale, and fell trembling and fainting to the ground, where she remained for some time, until revived by the care of her attendants. (See her *Life*).

Day 13

Jesus before the Tribunal of Pilate

Meditation

Pilate being well aware of the malice of the Jews, and that they are seeking the death of Jesus solely to satiate their anger and envy, asks them what accusations they bring against Him to form the subject of examination. Consider—

1.The falsity of the accusations brought against Jesus.

He is accused of being a seditious, turbulent man; and yet on no subject has He preached with so much zeal as on those relating to subordination, obedience and humility. In all His discourses He has inculcated no virtues with more ardor than meekness, submission and love of enemies. He is accused of having forbidden tribute to be paid to Caesar. But what dark malice must have suggested so odious a calumny to oppress His innocence, for His enemies are well aware that Christ paid the tribute Himself and for St. Peter! Be consoled, O you who are disciples of Jesus, whenever you are treated as was your Divine Master. You will resemble Him, if your enemies resemble His in their calumnies. The third accusation produced against Jesus, as involving a most heinous crime, is that He sought to make Himself king, and yet he never affected the outward appearance, or bore the insignia of one! His deportment has always been humble, submissive and simple, and whenever the people attempted to proclaim Him king, He always fled and concealed Himself. Oh, how many calumnies are invented by the perfidious Jews for the sake of depriving our most innocent Saviour of His honor and life! In the meantime, what is the demeanor of Jesus on beholding Himself thus falsely accused? He humbles Himself, and is silent. He loves these humiliations, and willingly embraces them to satisfy for our pride. Can anyone contemplate a Man-God thus unjustly calumniated before a public tribunal, and not willingly submit to a slight aspersion upon his own reputation and innocence?

2. The humility of Jesus throughout His examination.

The governor, having returned into his audience-chamber, summons Jesus into his

presence, that he may examine His case in private,
and with proper gravity, apart from any tumult. He
takes his seat as judge in his tribunal, and questions
Him, urging Him over and over again to answer,
and declare who and what He is. Represent to
yourself Jesus Christ standing as a criminal, with
His hands bound, and head bent downwards, before
a profane idolater, to be judged by him. So
profoundly does Jesus, the Son of God, the King of
Glory, the Judge of the Universe, humble Himself!
For three years He has been preaching humility, and
on this occasion, He preaches it more loudly and
efficaciously still, by His own example. Jesus Christ,
having replied to Pilate in a few words full of
heavenly wisdom, so as to refute all the accusations
brought against Him, maintains a profound
mysterious silence. The high priests grow warm in
the repetition of their exaggerated calumnies, and
the governor urges Him to prove His innocence. The
preservation of His Good name, and even of life,
seems now to call for self-defense. Nothing could be
more easy than for Jesus to prove His innocence,
and confound His enemies, and yet He is silent. He
holds His peace because His enemies are not worthy

again to hear His voice. He holds His peace, to teach us by His own example how to be silent and humble in adversity. He holds His peace, because He is not desirous of being set at liberty—because He is only sighing for the moment when He is to die for me. Oh, charity of my Jesus! Can I ever sufficiently praise Thee or worthily love Thee?

3. The innocence of Jesus proclaimed by the judge.

Pilate, having examined the cause of Jesus, finds Him innocent, and publicly declares that there is no guilt in Him. Our blessed Lord has been presented before three different tribunals, and in each His innocence has been found unsullied. And yet He is treated as a criminal and sentenced to punishment. Jesus is perfectly innocent, even by sentence of His judges; Jesus has done nought but good, and nevertheless He vouchsafes to subject Himself to punishment, as though He were the worst of malefactors, and I who am guilty of many sins, will not accept the slight penance of some little shame or suffering which Divine Justice inflicts upon me by the instrumentality of others. I have so many times deserved Hell on account of the innumerable sins which I have committed against my God. I am perfectly convinced and persuaded of this truth, and yet I cannot bear any trial sent me by Our Lord in expiation of my sins! How different is my conduct from Thine, O my Jesus! In Thy Passion Thou dost expiate faults not Thy own, and in all Thy sufferings I am ever present to Thy mind; while I have not courage to punish myself for my own sins, which have cost Thee so much, because I do not keep Thee, the Great Example of patience and penance, before my eyes.

THE FRUIT

Determine to love sincerely all those who calumniate or speak ill of you, making a sacrifice of all desires of vengeance to Jesus Christ. Learn from the example of Jesus to be silent on those occasions when it would be lawful or advantageous for you to speak in your own defense, and do this for the love of Him. Offer to God as a penance for your sins all the trials of this life, declaring your readiness to accept anything from the hands of God.

EXAMPLE

Saint Peter Martyr, a friar of the order of Preachers, being falsely accused to His superior of a heinous crime, and on that account severely rebuked and penanced, preserved a humble silence, and submitted with heroic resignation to the punishment inflicted on him. Now it happened one night while he was praying before his Crucifix that he began to reflect upon his innocence, and how he had been unjustly accused and penanced, so that his heart heaved with sorrow, and he sighed deeply, exclaiming to Jesus Crucified, with a view to give vent to his grief, "O Lord, Thou knowest my innocence, and why hast Thou permitted that calumny should prevail against me, and that I should be so unjustly treated?" Then Jesus answered from the Crucifix, "And what have I done, O Peter, to deserve to be thus nailed to a Cross? Learn from my example, to suffer with patience." These sweet words made the heart of the sorrowing Saint bound with joy, and inspired him with constancy and courage in suffering any tribulation for the love of his Crucified Jesus. (See his *Life*).

DAY 14

Jesus is Presented before Herod

MEDITATION

Pilate, having heard that Jesus was from Galilee, which belonged to the jurisdiction of Herod, to escape judging His cause, sent Him to that monarch, who was then dwelling in Jerusalem, that he might dispose of His sacred Person, as best suited him. Consider—

1. In what manner Herod receives Jesus.

The Jews are eager to conduct our blessed Lord to the house of Herod, because they hope that this barbarous king will pronounce sentence of death upon Him, and they likewise exercise their ingenuity in finding out new modes of afflicting Him with inhuman tortures during this His fourth most painful journey. Compassionate the Son of God under the new outrages, insults, and degradations to which He is exposed as He passes through the streets of Jerusalem. Herod, hearing of the approach of Jesus, rejoices, and receives Him on His arrival with feelings of hope, joy, and desire. But his joy is vain, for He rejoices solely at beholding a wonderful Man, and satisfying his curiosity, while he thinks but little of profiting by the presence of Christ for his soul's salvation. Thus it is that he sees Him, speaks to Him, and knows Him not, but remains in his sins. Rejoice when God visits and speaks to you in prayer, but be attentive for your soul to profit by the visits of your Lord. The desires of Herod are barren and unproductive. He has long desired to see Jesus, and yet he had never sought Him. He had already heard of the wonders wrought by His hand. He knew that the whole world was running after Him, and yet he would not go a step to see Jesus and profit by His preaching. Many there are who resemble Herod, who desire to do penance, to be converted and to save their souls, but who never make a firm resolution, and die before having begun the work of their conversion. The hope of Herod is impious. He hopes to see Jesus Christ work some miracle; he hopes to hear His teaching, and to be gratified by His eloquence, not for his soul's sake but to feed vanity and satisfy curiosity. Hence he is deceived in his expectations, and Jesus does not vouchsafe him a single word. Are you waiting for some miracle to be worked before you will resolve to love and serve God? God will not work one, and you will remain in sin.

2. The deportment of Jesus toward Herod.

Herod makes every effort to obtain some answer from Jesus. He questions Him in various ways, urging, and eagerly tempting Him to speak; but Jesus is silent, and although He perceives that His silence will expose Him to be treated as a fool or madman, and that if He speaks He will, on the contrary, be regarded as a wise man and please the prince, still He opens not His mouth and utters not a single word. He hears the high priests and scribes furiously maintaining their accusations against Him, and still He is silent. Oh, how admirable, how instructive is this silence of Jesus! Herod is filled with pride and malice, and God holds converse only with the humble, the meek, and the simple. Herod is defiled with the sin of adultery, and God speaks not to sullied and impure souls. Seek then to be humble, and preserve the greatest purity of heart, if you wish to be in a state to hear the voice of God. Herod has never made any effort to see Jesus, although he might easily have done so, and now Jesus refuses to speak to him. Such is the fate of all who despise the grace of God—by a just judgment it is refused them. Oh, how terrible a misfortune is the silence of God for a soul! How unhappy is that heart to which the Lord no longer speaks by His holy inspirations! Beware of rendering yourself unworthy of them, by turning a deaf ear to them, and by indulging your evil passions.

3. Jesus is treated with scorn in the court of Herod.

Herod being offended at the silence of Jesus, and enraged at finding himself deceived in his expectations, begins to deride Him by word and gesture, and to treat Him with scorn as a senseless, mad, deluded man. Behold, my soul the depth of humiliation to which the almighty Son of God is subjected, even to that of being publicly treated as a fool and madman. Understand now at least how great an evil thy pride must be, since to effect its cure, a God has been obliged thus to humble Himself! The high priests, soldiers, and people, following the example of Herod, emulate each other in despising Jesus Christ, in laughing and scoffing at His ignominious position, and insulting and deriding the degradation of His sacred Person. But in the meantime, our afflicted Redeemer, thus shamefully insulted by vile creatures, is silent and complains not. Truly this is a miracle of patience worthy of a God. A like miracle has God so frequently wrought in your regard, when He has with infinite patience and mercy borne with your sins. Herod, who had so eagerly desired to behold Christ, now despises Him, clothes Him in a white robe, that so He may be openly recognized as a fool, and sends Him back to Pilate. Accompany your blessed Lord with love and compassion through the crowded streets of the city. Everywhere, and by everyone is He shamefully outraged. There is not one to defend or assist Him amid so many insults and sufferings. He is the author of wisdom, and yet rejoices in being treated as a fool, to teach me that true wisdom consists in despising the judgments of the world, and in imitating His humility.

THE FRUIT

Begin at length in real earnest to love and serve God; you have lost time enough in offending Him. Place the greatest value on the graces and inspirations of Our Lord; your eternal salvation may depend upon your correspondence with or rejection of, one single grace. Take for your rule of life, not the maxims and opinions of the world, but the truths of the Gospel, and the example of Jesus Christ. The wisdom of the world is as folly before God, and truly wise are those who are reputed as fools of the world.

EXAMPLE

The lovers of Christ Crucified are always most anxious to awaken a spirit of devotion to His sufferings in the hearts of men. Such, from earliest youth, was the fervent desire of Saint Paul of the Cross, and having bound himself by vow to promote devotion to Christ Crucified by every means in his power, he made it the principal object of all his thoughts, actions, journeys, spiritual exercises, missions, discourses and writings. The very day of his death, being unable to speak, he took a little Crucifix into his hand, and with his eyes fervently expressed the feelings of his heart, so as to make known to a gentleman who had come to visit him, how the Passion of Jesus Christ should be ever present to his mind, and to impress this still more strongly upon him, he gave him the little Crucifix. You also may sometimes promote this devotion by a few pious words. (See his *Life*).

DAY 15

Barabbas Preferred Before Jesus

MEDITATION

Pilate finding no cause in Jesus, and being willing to save Him from His enemies, has recourse to the expedient of offering the people their choice between Him and Barabbas, who is a man so hateful to all on account of his crimes, that it does not seem possible they can for a moment hesitate to ask the favor for Jesus Christ. Consider—

1. The insult Pilate offers Jesus by comparing Him with Barabbas.

Who is Jesus, and who is Barabbas? Jesus is the Eternal Son of God, the King of Majesty, the Lord of Glory, the Creator of Heaven and Earth and the Holy of Holies. It would be a grievous insult to compare Him with the highest of the Angels, what then must it be to compare Him with Barabbas, a rebel, a thief, a murderer, and a notorious criminal? How keenly must the Heart of Jesus feel so ignominious of comparison! What anguish must his soul suffer on hearing Pilate say to the people:

"Which of the two will you have? Whom do you prefer? Whom do you love best, Jesus or Barabbas?" And yet He joyfully submits even to this disgraceful outrage. How often have you renewed this shameful comparison? Whenever the devil has tempted you to indulge in some sensual pleasure, or the world has instigated you to take vengeance, and you have been careless and lukewarm in rejecting the temptation, being undecided as to whether it were better to please God and obey His laws, or indulge your evil passions, so often have you compared God, the Sovereign Infinite Good, to a miserable gratification and vile pleasure. What an outrage to God! What an insult to His Majesty! Be ashamed of your rash presumption, and weep over your sin.

2. The unjust preference given by the Jews to Barabbas.

The Jews having heard the proposal of Pilate, and being inflamed with rage against our innocent Saviour, exclaim as one man, *"Not Jesus, but Barabbas!"* They are well aware of the unsullied innocence of Jesus—they have been witnesses of the sanctity of His life—they have received infinite benefits from His hand, nay, many out of that numerous crowd have been miraculously healed by Him. And yet, though a prodigy of injustice, there is not one man in all that multitude who will ask for His liberation! And the most generous of benefactors is set aside for the sake of a wicked seditious man! The God of Majesty and Holiness is treated as nought in comparison with a murderer! Words can never describe how deep a wound is inflicted on the loving Heart of Jesus by the intolerable injustice done Him on this occasion by His chosen people. Compassionate Him in this His painful humiliation, but pause and reflect also upon your own conduct. The Jews are guilty in preferring Barabbas before Jesus, but they committed this enormous crime upon one occasion only, whereas how many times have you exclaimed in your heart, by consenting to sin, "Away with God from my soul, give unto me the devil with that wicked pleasure, or illicit gain, or that gratification of my evil passions!" You have preferred the devil to Jesus whenever you have renounced the service of God. You knew that Jesus was your King, you believed Him to be your God, you adored Him as your Saviour, and yet you thus preferred an unclean and degrading sensual pleasure before Him! What more frightful injustice than this? Detest your malice, force your perverse will to retract its shameful determinations, and resolve ever to prefer God before all created objects.

3. The Jews having asked for the liberation of Barabbas—thus proving that they set more value on the life of a public thief, than on that of the Saviour of the world, now demand with loud cries that Jesus should be condemned, that He should be put to death, that He should be crucified.

Who could have thought that this ungrateful people would have reached such a height of iniquity as to desire the crucifixion of their King, their Messias, and their Deliverer—the Expectation of Nations, whose presence they had so long sighed for, and whom, but a few days before, they had welcomed with acclamations as the Son of God? But who would ever believe that a Christian, so liberally loaded with favors, so tenderly loved by Jesus, could commit so atrocious a crime as to explain in his heart, *"Let Jesus die!"* And yet such is your daily cry by the commission of mortal sin. You say, not with your voice, but by your deeds: *"Let sin triumph, but let Jesus die! The loss of God I consent to, but not the loss of this shameful pleasure. Let Jesus be crucified, and sin reign in my soul."* Can any impiety or ingratitude surpass this? Pilate says to the furious Jews: *"But what evil hath Jesus done,* that you wish Him to die?" And they persist in crying, *"Let Him be crucified!"* "What evil hath Jesus done you," was the cry also of your conscience, "that you are determined to offend Him?" And yet you obstinately persisted in sin, and in crucifying Jesus. The only crime of Jesus is that of too much love for us, His charity has induced Him willingly to accept death for our sakes. His love for you, and desire for your salvation, cause Him to wait for you with such infinite patience, even after all the outrages you have committed against Him. Love so loving a God, thank so merciful a God, and displease not so good a God any more.

THE FRUIT

Determine to avoid sin above every other evil. Be careful and prompt in banishing bad thoughts and the wicked suggestions of the devil, declaring your firm determination of serving God alone. Conceive a holy hatred against your flesh, your passions, and your self-love, which have so frequently caused you to offend God. Often say of these enemies, *"Let them be crucified!"* and endeavor to crucify them by mortification.

EXAMPLE

There is nothing which may not serve to remind the lovers of Christ Crucified of the sufferings and death of their beloved Redeemer. The servant of God, Sister Mary Minima, of Jesus of Nazareth, a Carmelite nun, was one Friday in March sitting down to table, when she saw a little lamb come into the Refectory, run towards her and take refuge in her arms. More was not required to make her think of Jesus, the Lamb without spot, delivered up by the furious Jews to the bitterest torments and most ignominious death. She was so much overcome by this reflection, and so many tears flowed from her eyes, that she was quite unable to take any food for the remainder of the day.

Accustom yourself in like manner to take occasion from everything to remember the sufferings of Jesus. (See her *Life*).

Day 16

Jesus Scourged at the Pillar

Meditation

Pilate, perceiving the obstinacy of the people in requiring that Jesus should be crucified, sentenced Him, in the first place, to the shameful punishment of scourging, and consigned Him to the hands of the soldiers, that his orders might be executed. Consider—

1. Jesus before the scourging.

The soldiers having received orders to scourge Jesus Christ, fall furiously upon Him, and lead Him to the public place where it is customary to flagellate the lowest criminals. The Jews rejoice at seeing their hated Saviour at length condemned to so dreadful a punishment, but Jesus rejoices even more at beholding the long sighed for hour arrived at last, in which He is to shed His Blood for my salvation through the instrumentality of the scourges. He is consumed with an ardent desire of suffering for my sake, and therefore it is that He allows Himself to be led by His executioners wherever they will, and offers not the slightest resistance. Learn to accept with patience all the sufferings God sends you in expiation of your sins. Jesus being arrived at the spot appointed, His enemies fall upon Him with the fury of wild beasts, unbind His chains, strip off His clothes, and, binding Him tightly to a pillar, expose Him in this state of nakedness and humiliation to the sight and undisguised scorn of the insolent rabble. Oh, what ignominy, what shame, what painful confusion must our blessed Jesus have experienced on beholding His virginal purity thus exposed to the derision and insults of a large crowd of people! And yet He endures everything in silence, and offers all with infinite charity to His Eternal Father, in satisfaction for my sins of immodesty and pride. The force of love alone is sufficient to bind Him to that pillar, ready and willing to submit to the scourges, and to shed every drop of His Blood. O beloved Son of God! I thank Thee for such infinite charity.

2. Jesus during the time of scourging.

The executioners having prepared instruments proper for the purpose of inflicting intense suffering on Jesus, now strike that virginal and immaculate flesh with unparalleled fierceness and cruelty. That most Holy Body is soon all wounds. From the top of His head down to the soles of the feet, it is so lacerated that at length all the bones may be counted. And yet out of all the vast number of persons who behold this heart-rending sight, there is not one to compassionate our suffering Jesus. Hard indeed must your heart be if it be not moved to compassion at the sight of your blessed Lord enduring such a martyrdom. The executioners continue to strike Him, encouraging one another in their cruel labor. Wound succeeds wound, the suffering thus inflicted becomes more and more acute, and the Body of Jesus is one entire wound. The scourges fall heavily upon His tender limbs, tearing, rending, and even carrying away portions of the flesh, which fall on all sides. The blood flows in streams, blood bathes the whole person of our blessed Redeemer, blood trickles down the pillar, blood soaks the earth, and blood is sprinkled on the executioners, who feel no emotions of pity even at such a sight. The cruelty of the executioners is at length exhausted, but the patience of Jesus wearies not; He suffers excruciating torments, it is true, and each blow inflicts fresh torture, alone sufficient to cause His death, but yet He rejoices to shed so much blood, to suffer agony so unspeakable, to give us incontestable proofs of the greatness of His love for us, and to show us the enormity of sin. Jesus is scourged, for no crime of His own, but to expiate, in His innocent flesh, those sins of impurity with which you have so often defiled your body. Contemplate Jesus at the pillar, bleeding and lacerated from head to foot, and learn hence all that your sins of impurity have cost Him. Beseech Him to cleanse all the stains of your soul with His divine Blood.

3. Jesus after the scourging.

The executioners, weary of inflicting further torture upon Jesus, unbind Him from the pillar, and He, unable from exhaustion and excess of suffering to support Himself on His feet, falls to the ground bathed in His own Precious Blood. Ah, who would not have been touched at so mournful a sight? The Jews alone feel no compassion for Jesus. Behold, my soul, behold thy loving Redeemer lying prostrate and almost powerless, on the ground, and recognize in His Wounds the effect of thy sins, and of the excess of His charity, which has thus opened to thee new sources of grace. Compassionate Him who has suffered so much for thy sake, and love Him who has so much loved thee. Draw near to Jesus as He lies bleeding on the ground, with no one to assist Him to rise, and do thou afford His afflicted Heart some relief by the affections of thine. See with what meekness He endures the derision and contempt of His enemies in this His state of humiliation and suffering. Acknowledge how deeply thou art indebted to Jesus, who has bestowed on thee a bath of His own most precious Blood in which thou mayest cleanse thy corrupted sores, and who, by so plentiful a Redemption, has delivered thee from the eternal maledictions thy sins deserved.

THE FRUIT

Resolve to endure any inconvenience which may befall you, and to deprive yourself of some lawful gratification, in punishment of your sins, which have cost Jesus so dear. Determine upon what particular points you will mortify yourself, and take great care to mortify those senses by which you have so often offended God. And offer to Jesus tears of sincere repentance for your sins, and of loving compassion for His sufferings, as some slight testimony of gratitude for all the Blood which He has shed for you.

EXAMPLE

Blessed Serafino d'Ascoli, a Capuchin Friar, not satisfied with spending whole nights in meditating on the Passion of Christ, passing entire weeks almost without food for love of Him, and paying his suffering Lord the tribute of plentiful tears and sighs, offered Him, moreover, the sacrifice of his own blood. When meditating on Jesus scourged at the pillar, he would enter into so holy an indignation against himself, scourge his body so severely, and draw forth such streams of blood, through his love of Christ, and through his great desire of resembling Him, that he seemed bent on rendering his body one wound, like that of Jesus in His scourging, Jesus Christ asks not so much of you, but at least do not refuse to endure some slight penance for love of Him.

DAY 17

Jesus is Crowned with Thorn

MEDITATION

The soldiers, having scourged Jesus, are inspired by the devil with a new method of torturing Him. They take a bundle of long, sharp, strong thorns, and having woven them into a crown, place it on His head, thus constituting Him the King of ignominy and suffering. Consider—

1. The inexpressible agony inflicted by this torture.

If a single thorn were to pierce your head, what exquisite pain would it not cause? But if it were ever so slightly pressed, the anguish would become quite insupportable. The sacred Head of Jesus is encircled with a whole wreath of long sharp thorns which pierce it on every side. Oh, what torture must our suffering Redeemer now experience. Behold what your impure thoughts, guilty pleasures, and sinful desires have cost Jesus! Behold by what exquisite sufferings Jesus has expiated your ambitious designs, your vanity, and your pride, and at how

dear a rate he has purchased for you the graces of
humility, patience and contempt of the world! The
barbarous soldiers, eager to inflict all possible
torture upon our patient Saviour, violently press
down the crown upon His brow, by repeated blows,
so that the sharp thorns wound and pierce the most
delicate parts of that adorable Head. My soul,
contemplate this King of Sorrows, and behold the
streams of blood flowing from every part of His
wounded Head, disfiguring and discoloring His
amiable countenance. Oh, how much blood has thy
salvation cost Jesus! Compassionate thy suffering
Redeemer, and recognize the fruit of thy hateful sins
in those thorns, those wounds, and those streams of
blood. Each time that thou hast deliberately
entertained evil thoughts, so often hast thou
crowned the sacred Head of Jesus with sharp thorns.
Is it possible that thou canst ever more indulge in
vain, blasphemous, and impure thoughts, or in
desires of earthly grandeur, after reflecting upon
Jesus crowned with thorns?

2. The disgraceful character of this torture.

The enemies of Jesus Christ seem to take
peculiar satisfaction in making Him a mock King, in

ridiculing His sufferings, and in subjecting Him to every species of degradation and insult. They furiously tear off His garments, and clothe Him in a ragged purple mantle. This outrage is a source of exquisite suffering to Jesus, for the tearing off His garments re-opens all the wounds which have been so lately inflicted by His flagellation, so that fresh blood flows from the lacerated limbs. Oh, how much have the pleasures of our sinful flesh, the delicacy of our bodies, the luxury and vanity of our clothing, cost our sweet Jesus!

They place in His hand a reed as a scepter, to constitute Him a mock King, a King of a theater! Jesus refuses it not, but receives and holds it in His hand, rejoicing by so great a dishonor to merit for you graces of strength and perseverance in virtue, and to purchase for you a heavenly kingdom. In this state Jesus appears to the insolent soldiery a proper subject for mockery, and they proceed to ridicule Him in a manner worthy of their cruelty. They all march before Him, saluting Him in the most derisive terms King of the Jews. They deride Him as a wretched imposter, adding shameful insults and reproaches to the most humiliating expressions of scorn and ridicule; they spit in His face, give him blows, and, taking the reed out of His hand, strike the crown of thorns with it so violently as to enlarge every wound, and cause Him the most exquisite pain. They vie with each other in deriding and insulting Him, and in rendering His sufferings yet more cruel and ignominious. Oh, how ingenious is human cruelty in torturing Jesus! But, in the meantime, His most holy Soul, though overwhelmed with the weight of so much ignominy and suffering, rejoices in offering to His Eternal Father the sacrifice of humiliations so profound in reparation of the outrages offered to His Majesty by our sins. Bow down in adoration before this Divine King, return Him thanks for His infinite charity, and promise that you will love Him alone for the remainder of your life.

3. The patience of Jesus.

Amid His bitterest sufferings and most excessive humiliations, Jesus never once opens His mouth to complain. A frightful crown of thorns pierces His head on every side, and causes Him the acutest pain, yet he makes not the slightest complaint of the cruelty of His enemies. What do you say to this example of divine and superhuman patience, O you who are ever seeking after worldly pleasures and sensual gratifications, and who cannot endure even the slight thorn of some small inconvenience or trifling pain? You ought indeed to feel ashamed of living in luxury, when you behold your King, your Creator, and your God crowned with sorrow and ignominy. Do you calculate upon entering Heaven crowned with the roses of pleasure instead of the thorns of mortification, suffering, and penance? Deceptive hope! Jesus Christ beholds Himself abandoned by all—in the power of His cruel enemies, outraged, defied with spittle, buffeted, and smitten, yet He maintains peace of soul, and calmness of demeanor, and makes not the slightest gesture of anger or impatience. And you, wretched worm of the earth, unworthy sinner—you have not yet learned to submit in peace and silence to an insult, injury, or wrong done you by your neighbors! Is it possible that the sight of a God thus loaded with ignominy and suffering, and yet so patient and so humble, should not be sufficient to teach you patience and humility? If you do not imitate the example of Jesus Christ, you will not partake of His glory.

THE FRUIT

On all those occasions when it is your lot to suffer some inconvenience, annoyance, or illness, or any mortification of your senses and inclinations, imagine that Jesus offers you one of His thorns, and willingly accept and submit to it for love of Him. In time of temptation, and when assailed by evil thoughts, remember Jesus crowned with thorns, cast your eyes mentally upon His pierced head, and resolve that you will never renew His sufferings.

EXAMPLE

A soul that loves Christ Crucified is ingenious in discovering ways of suffering in imitation of Him. When Saint Paul of the Cross was walking without shoes or stockings through wild and stony paths, sharp thorns would often enter his feet, and he would allow them to run in deeply, being well satisfied to suffer acute pain for the love of his Crucified Lord. Sometimes one of his companions would perceive what had happened, and, being anxious to relieve his pain, would express sorrow for it, and offer to extract the thorn. But then the servant of God would answer that what he suffered was nothing, since Jesus his Redeemer had permitted so many sharp thorns to transfix His most sacred Head. (See his *Life*).

Day 18

Jesus Christ shown by Pilate to the People

Meditation

Pilate, on beholding the Redeemer of the world in the lamentable condition to which His executioners have reduced Him, imagines that His appearance alone must move the people to compassion, and therefore takes Him to the balcony in front of his palace, from whence He may be seen by the assembled multitude, saying *"Ecce Homo." — "Behold the Man!"* Consider—

1. The state in which Jesus is shown to the people.

He is so deformed and disfigured as scarcely to preserve the semblance of a man. His face is pale and bruised with the blows He has received, and defiled with the spittle—His adorable head is bending beneath the painful weight of the sharp thorns, which pierce His brow and form a crown of sorrow and ignominy—His torn, mangled, and bleeding frame is clothed with a garment of scorn and derision. He suffers in every part of His sacred

Body, and His position is one of the deepest degradation. In this state of indescribable shame and confusion, the adorable Son of God is presented by Pilate to the people with these few words: *"Behold the Man!"* As though he had said: "Behold to what a condition the Man whom you accuse of aspiring to royalty is reduced! See whether He is not rather worthy of tears and compassion than of hatred!" And thou, my soul, attentively contemplate this Man-God, the King of Glory, overwhelmed with ignominy, in the presence of so great a multitude, His adorable Body streaming with blood and loaded with shame. He who was the most beautiful of the sons of men, is now the abomination of His people. He has assumed so painful and humiliating an appearance to induce His Father to take pity upon us, and deliver us from the eternal punishments which we have deserved. Love for our souls, and desire for their salvation, have reduced Him to so pitiable a condition. But, on your part, what efforts do you make for the salvation of your soul which has been purchased by Jesus at so dear a rate? Are you anxious to guard its purity and save it from eternal misery? Or are you, on the contrary, willing for a mere trifle to sacrifice your right to that Paradise which Jesus has purchased for you at the price of so many humiliations and sufferings?

2. The feelings aroused in the hearts of the people by the appearance of Jesus.

The sight of the lamentable condition to which the most innocent Redeemer of the world is reduced, would have touched hearts of stone, and ought to inspire the Jews with feelings of compassion and mercy toward our suffering Jesus. But no sooner do they behold Him than they seem to lose every feeling of humanity, and, with the fury of wild beasts, clamorously demand His death, and seek with unexampled fury to deprive Him of that life which is all but extinct in His martyred Body. The diabolical hatred and implacable rage animating them against our blessed Lord urge them on to demand with loud cries *that He should be crucified!* Behold the consequences of allowing a passion once to take possession of the heart! There is no excess into which a man blinded by any one passion may not fall. All passions delight but ruin the soul, and must therefore be combated with untiring energy. Pilate is well aware of the innocence of Jesus, and is by no means willing to yield to the iniquitous wishes of the Jews, but they fiercely and clamorously reply that *according to their law* He ought to die, because He has made Himself the son of God. The laws of the world condemn Jesus to die. All worldlings who seek solely to gratify their passions exclaim by the voice of the Jews that Jesus must be put to death, that Jesus must be crucified! And do you regulate your conduct by such laws as these? Do you follow the maxims of worldlings? If such is the case, you will very speedily desert Jesus, and seek to crucify Him anew. Jesus beholds the rage of His enemies, He hears their furious outcries, and bitterly deplores their insensibility to His sufferings, but rejoices at the prospect of that Cross on which He is to die for love of me, while I tremble at the very name of crosses and sufferings. Why are my sentiments so contrary to those of Jesus?

3. The feelings which the sight of Jesus Christ should awaken in our hearts.

While the people display no compassion whatever on beholding Jesus, let us imagine that the Eternal Father shows Him to us to excite at least in our hearts feelings of love, veneration, and of desire to imitate Him. Let us imagine that we hear the Eternal Father addressing us in the words of Pilate to the Jews, *"Ecce Homo"*—*"Behold the Man!"* He is your King, the King of wisdom, of love, and of holiness, but also the King of sorrow and ignominy. He has acquired possession of His kingdom by humiliation and suffering; He has purchased it for you at the price of His Blood and of His Wounds: for your sake He has sacrificed His dignity, and permitted Himself to be thus outraged and tormented. Adore this King, be subject to Him, and if you wish to enter His blessed Kingdom, follow Him in the way of the Cross and of suffering. He is desirous of reigning in your hearts, and He has purchased possession of them at the price of a most painful death. Consecrate then to Him all your thoughts and all your affections. *Behold the Man!* He is your Father; the most sweet, tender and loving of fathers—a Father who, for the love of His children, and in order to restore them to the life of grace which they had lost by sin, has sacrificed His own most precious life on the Cross, and is yet the most despised and abhorred of fathers. Love so good a Father, obey His commands, and never grieve His tender Heart. *Behold the Man!* He is your Master and your Model. Observe the virtues which He practices on this occasion. Extreme mildness amid so many provocations, perfect silence under so many outrages, great humility amid so many insults, and wonderful patience under so many sufferings. Contemplate, and endeavor to imitate Him. Never will you resemble Him in the honors of Paradise, never will you be His companions in glory, if you resemble Him not in His virtues. Resolve to do so by the help of His grace.

THE FRUIT

Remain for some time with your eyes fixed on a Crucifix, and say to yourself, "Behold the condition to which a God has been reduced for love of me, and to satisfy for my sins." Offer Him all the powers of your soul, and all the senses of your body, in testimony of your love, and determine to use them solely for His glory. Ask Him, through the merits of His humiliations, to bestow upon you the spirit of humility and penance.

EXAMPLE

The venerable servant of God, Ursula Benincasa, took such great delight in having constantly before her eyes a picture representing Jesus crowned with thorns, and in the state in which He was shown by Pilate to the people, that she had it fastened on her working frame. When working she would frequently breathe forth fervent sighs of love to her suffering Lord, and beseech Him to allow her to partake in His sorrows, and to share His crown of thorns. She caused Crucifixes to be placed in every part of her house, and kept many in her room, so that, whichever way she turned, she might always behold her suffering Redeemer. Having become a Religious, and Superior of a Convent, she ordered each of her nuns to keep in her cell an image of Christ Crucified, and to say at least thirty-three times ever day, *"My Crucified Jesus! I repent of all my sins. Have mercy on me, and help me at the hour of my death."* (See her *Life*).

DAY 19

Jesus Condemned to the Death of the Cross

MEDITATION

Pilate, seeing that he gains nothing by all his attempts to liberate Jesus, but that, on the contrary, the people are being excited by the high priests to demand that He should be crucified, at last makes up his mind to pronounce sentence, and condemn Our Saviour to the death of the Cross. Consider—

1. The people desire the death of Jesus.

The Jews are not satisfied with the scourging of Jesus, nor yet with His crowning with thorns, nor with His having been overwhelmed with disgrace and ignominy; they require nothing less than his death, and urge Pilate to have Him crucified. You also have desired His death as often as you have sinned, and the voice of your perfidious, malicious will has uttered the cry, *Crucifige*, against your tender Father, Saviour and God, as loudly as ever the Jews did! Oh, what ingratitude and cruelty!

The Jews had sought for Jesus to make Him king; they had experienced the effects of His beneficence; they had received the most signal favors from His hand, both for soul and body; and now with unexampled ingratitude they demand that He should be put to death on the Cross like a malefactor, and cannot even endure the sight of His adorable Person. Hence they desire Pilate to *take Him away*; as though they had said, "We cannot longer endure to behold Him, so hateful and disagreeable is His presence to us!" This is always the aim of the wicked. They have no wish to know God, or to contemplate His infinite perfections, and they will not reflect upon His benefits, goodness and love for us. If they once did so, they would have no difficulty in abstaining from sin. The sight of Jesus reminded the Jews of His miracles and beneficence, and was a reproach to them for their atrocious injustice and fearful ingratitude in desiring His death. On this account they would not look at Him whose appearance aroused remorse in their hearts. You commit sin, offend God, and persecute Jesus even unto death, because you never will pause and consider how much Jesus has loved you, nor how much He has suffered for your sake. You live in forgetfulness of God, with scarcely any knowledge of Him, immersed in vanity and idle curiosity, and absolutely unmindful of your loving Benefactor and Sovereign Good; hence it follows that you feel no horror of crying out, by your hateful sins, that He must be crucified, that He must die. And what has Jesus done to deserve such treatment at your hands?

2. Pilate condemns Jesus.

Pilate would willingly liberate Jesus, but his courage fails him. He fears to condemn Him because the thought of His evident innocence causes him to tremble. And yet when he hears the people threaten him with the anger of Caesar, Pilate betrays his conscience, and condemns the Just Man, the Holy of Holies, to death, delivering Him up into the hands of His most furious enemies! O accursed human respect! How many times have you, O Christian, put the Son of God to death in your heart by committing sin through human respect? Not to displease a friend, not to lose the favor of a person who is agreeable to you, not to be deprived of some vain transitory honor, not to lose some wretched pleasure, you have committed the monstrous evil of offending God! And yet you knew that He was your Lord, that He had a right to be obeyed and preferred by you to all things else. You knew that He commanded you to sacrifice friends and inclinations alike to His will and law. How is it possible that you have made more account of a creature than of God, and that, through human respect and fear of men, you have renounced the friendship of God your Father? How is it possible that you can have been more afraid of displeasing men than of outraging the infinite Majesty of God by sin? Bewail your error, and hold human respect in detestation. Pilate trembles and is filled with horror when pronouncing sentence of death against the God of life; yet all his knowledge, remorse of conscience, and the evident proofs he has of the innocence of Jesus, are not sufficient to restrain him from committing so awful a crime, and he consents to the deicide. Indulge in no feelings of anger against Pilate, but rather turn them against yourself, who, in despite of the light of faith, the assistance of grace, and remorse of conscience, have sentenced Jesus Christ to death each time that you have committed mortal sin. And ought not the mere remembrance of this to cause you to die of grief?

3. Jesus Christ accepts death.

Jesus is standing in the position of a criminal before the tribunal of Pilate, while His sentence of death is pronounced. He hears the iniquitous decree by which He is condemned to die as a malefactor upon a Cross, and, reverently bowing down His Divine head, He submissively accepts it, without making the slightest opposition. He complains not of the wrong done Him; He appeals not to the judge who is abandoning Him to the rage of His most cruel enemies; He murmurs not at the injustice of the sentence, and He utters not one word in His own defense, but willingly and joyfully accepts death, for the glory of His Father and for love of us. Do you manifest equal obedience and submission to the orders of Providence, and to the designs of God in your regard? The sacrifices the Almighty requires of you will never be so arduous as to equal the bitterness and ignominy of the sentence of death pronounced against Jesus, and submitted to by Him for love of you, and to save you from eternal death. And cannot you for the love of Jesus accept that trial, or that humiliation, which is death to your self-love and pride? Oh, how great is your ingratitude toward One who has so much loved you! Jesus hears His enemies triumphing and rejoicing at His condemnation to death, and deeply as His most holy Heart grieves over their perfidious malice, yet equally, nay, even far more, does He rejoice at beholding at hand the long sighed-for moment in which He is to sacrifice His life for our salvation. O how deeply are we indebted to our dear Redeemer! How much ought we to love Him who for love of us willingly consents to die upon a Cross! O my sweet Jesus, now at least may I begin in very truth to love Thee!

THE FRUIT

Human respect, and your own passions, have caused you to become so often, like the Jews, a rebel to your God. Resolve, then, to be vigilant in mortifying your passions, and in despising all human respect, when the good pleasure of God is in question. Never forget your God, the benefits you have received from His hand, His love and His sufferings. Pious thoughts such as these will prevent you from committing sin. Pay great attention to Divine inspirations, and to remorse of conscience, for they are graces by which God proposes either to save you from consenting to sin, or to raise you up if you have fallen.

EXAMPLE

Tears shed over the Passion of Our Lord are very pleasing to Him. Blessed Johanna of the Cross, who was filled with devotion to the sufferings of Jesus, even from her mother's womb (as was evident from the fact that, while yet a babe, she refused the breast on Fridays), was one day contemplating in spirit the streams of Blood which flowed down the sacred Body of her Crucified Redeemer, and lamenting that it was not granted to her to shed at least a portion of her blood for love of Him who, for her sake, had shed every drop of His, when an Angel appeared, and bade her be comforted, for that Our Lord regarded all the tears shed over His Passion in the light of so many drops of blood. (See her *Life*).

Day 20

Jesus Carries His Cross to Mount Calvary

Meditation

No sooner is Jesus Christ condemned to death, than He is delivered up to the Jews to be crucified. A Cross is hastily prepared, and placed on the shoulders of our Blessed Lord, who issues forth from Jerusalem, bearing that heavy burden, on the road to Calvary. Consider—

1. The manner in which Jesus accepts His Cross.

The soldiers, before placing the Cross upon the shoulders of Jesus, tear off the ragged purple mantle which He has worn until then, and *put on Him His own clothes again*, that He may be more easily recognized by all beholders. Thus are the wounds of Jesus re-opened, and the suffering and agony He endures are great in proportion to the length of time during which the mantle has adhered to His open wounds. Can we meditate upon this point of the Passion without pitying our most afflicted Redeemer, who suffers with such admirable patience and humility? For His greater torment, the crown of thorns is left upon His head, and oh, what a continual source of suffering is this crown to Him! The pressure of the Cross against His sacred Head, every movement He makes, and every step He takes, inflict the most acute torture upon Him. And yet Jesus utters not one word of complaint, but wears this painful crown even to His last breath. Be ashamed of your delicacy and unwillingness to endure the slightest trial. All things being thus arranged, and Jesus clothed in His seamless garment, the long and heavy Cross, upon which He is to be nailed, is presented to Him. Jesus lifts His eyes, and beholds it, and as it has ever been the object of His most loving desires, He embraces and tenderly presses it to His bosom; then, exhausted as He is, suffering, weak from loss of blood, and in a condition more nearly resembling death than life, places it upon His trembling, bleeding shoulders. Learn, O my soul, in what manner thou shouldst accept whatever God sends thee. It may be a heavy Cross that He sends thee, but remember that it is imposed upon thee by God Himself. Thou wilt never be called upon to suffer as much as Jesus, and unless thou bearest thy Cross after Him, thou wilt never partake of His glory

2. The ignominious manner in which Jesus comes forth from the Praetorium.

The Jews hasten to conduct Jesus to death, and in order to satisfy their hatred against the innocent Saviour of the world, they determine that He shall die in the company of malefactors, and thus be supposed to be equal to them in guilt. They therefore immediately bring forward two condemned robbers, and having placed Jesus between them, set forward in procession towards Mount Calvary. The people, hearing the cries of joy and loud acclamations of the soldiers hasten from all sides to behold the mournful spectacle.

Jesus comes forth from the Praetorium, between the two thieves who are His companions in punishment, bound with cords, His sacred Face defiled with blood and spittle, His Head crowned with thorns, and His adorable form bending beneath the heavy weight of the Cross which He is bearing with difficulty upon His shoulders. With what confusion must Jesus have been overwhelmed at being seen by everyone in so disgraceful a position!

How indescribably painful for Him, to whom sin is infinitely odious, to be exhibited to all Jerusalem in the character of a criminal about to suffer the penalty of his crimes! And yet He carries His Cross, and submits to the disgrace with so much patience and humility, with such meekness and mildness, that any hearts but those of the hardened Jews would have been touched with compassion.

Jesus, in taking up His Cross, has at the same time taken upon Himself all our sins; and it is to make satisfaction for them that He now willingly embraces this humiliation, and joyfully bears the heavy weight of the wood on which He is to sacrifice His life. Is it not just that you, who are guilty of so many faults by which you have immeasurably increased the weight of the Cross of Christ, and inflicted so much suffering upon Him, should now humbly and submissively bear the Cross of penance and of obedience to the Divine commands? All the streets of the city through which Jesus passes are crowded with people. Everyone watches, and takes pleasure in deriding and insulting Him in His sufferings. All blaspheme Him in the most derisive and disgraceful terms, and there is none to console, comfort, or assist Him. Approach, my soul, approach thy afflicted Redeemer, and by the light of faith recognize in that Man who is thus become the scorn of the people, thy Saviour, thy Father, and thy God, bearing in His own Person the penalty due to thy crimes; shed tears of contrition at His feet, and beware of increasing the weight of His Cross, and inflicting new sorrow upon His tender Heart by committing sin afresh.

3. The unspeakable agony He suffers during this His last journey.

Jesus being much weakened by all the Blood He has shed, is forced to exert the whole of His remaining strength to support the weight of the Cross, and every step He takes adds to His sufferings. He thus ascends the mount, sinking with fatigue, exhausted, and covered with wounds, but no one expresses any compassion for Him. He advances with the utmost difficulty, bearing on His weak and wounded shoulders that heavy Cross, which overpowers Him by its weight, and re-opens all His wounds, so that the traces of His passage are marked in Blood. Oh, what exquisite torture does our sweet Jesus now endure! Your unworthy

pleasures, and the steps you have taken in the paths
of iniquity, are the causes of all His sufferings. The
executioners strike, and force Him onward with
cruel blows; the strength of Jesus fails at length
entirely, and, overpowered by excessive suffering
and fatigue. He sinks beneath the heavy weight of
the Cross. My soul, attentively contemplate thy
Saviour falling beneath His Cross, and acknowledge
the enormity of thy sins. None but a Man-God could
bear their weight, and even He is overwhelmed with
the horror and deformity of so hateful a burden. If
thou hadst not sinned, the weight borne by Jesus
would have been less overpowering. The weight of
our sins inflicts more suffering upon Him than His
heavy Cross. Compassionate thy Lord thus
oppressed with sorrow on account of thy sins.

Jesus having risen from the ground, feels His
strength completely failing, and that He can do no
more. And yet, He must proceed onward to Mount
Calvary! His love for us, and desire to die for our
salvation, infuse vigor into that Body now nearly
drained of the last drop of Blood. He is sighing for
that moment in which He is to offer Himself as a
sacrifice to the honor of His Father, and for the

redemption of His brethren. O most sweet Jesus! such then is Thy love for me, and shall I still remain insensible and ungrateful to Thee?

THE FRUIT

There are crosses to be found everywhere, even upon the throne. Seek not to remove or avoid them, and bear them not unwillingly, but, on the contrary, endeavor to render them meritorious. The Cross alone conducts to Heaven, and there is no saint who has not loved it. Therefore, when an affliction or trial befall you, never fail to return God thanks, and let it be your study then to practice the virtues of humility, patience, and resignation, in imitation of Jesus bearing His Cross. Are you desirous of carrying your cross with ease? Carry it in the company of Jesus Christ.

EXAMPLE

There is no devotion dearer to the lovers of Jesus suffering than that commonly called the *Via Crucis*, the *Way of the Cross*. The servant of God, Sister Mary Minima, of Jesus of Nazareth, used to make the Way of the Cross, if possible, every day, shedding floods of tears, and deeply bewailing the sufferings of her Lord, whom she accompanied in spirit through the whole of His painful journey to Mount Calvary. One day, as she was performing this devotion, and meditating upon Jesus bearing His Cross, she heard Him say to her, *"Look upon Me; assist Me: love me."* From which circumstance her heart became inflamed with the most eager desire to relieve Jesus in His excessive sufferings. Do you also perform this devotion in a spirit of loving compassion for your suffering Lord? (See her *Life*).

DAY 21

The Meeting between Jesus and His Blessed Mother

MEDITATION

Our blessed Redeemer, on His way to Calvary, has an interview with His most holy Mother, who is following Him, together with the other holy women. Consider—

1. The anguish of heart experienced by Jesus at the sight of Mary.

He beholds her sorrowing, weeping, overwhelmed with the bitterest grief, and when the eyes of the Mother and of the Son meet, how deep a wound is inflicted on the tender Heart of Jesus! Jesus loves Mary as His Mother. Jesus, the most loving of Sons, entertains the most indescribable feelings of affection for Mary, the most amiable of mothers. How great, then, and how bitter must be His grief at beholding this beloved Mother so deeply afflicted and anguish-stricken on His account? Oh, hard indeed must that heart be which does not compassionate Jesus in this new suffering! The Cross of Jesus is heavy, His adorable Body is one single wound, but His Heart is transfixed with a sword of still deeper and more painful sorrow, from beholding the interior of the heart of Mary, in which love and compassion imprint, as in a clear mirror all His wounds, His thorns, His Cross, and His sufferings, and thus inflict the keenest anguish. What mind can conceive the indescribable sorrow experienced by the Heart of Jesus at this mournful spectacle! He would willingly bestow upon His Mother a last token of affection, speak one word of comfort to her sorrowing heart, and bid her a last farewell, but the fury of the Jews does not permit Him to linger one moment by her side. But if these two most holy personages speak not with their lips, their eyes and hearts certainly are not silent, but communicate to one another their mutual sorrows. Beseech Jesus to give you a share in His sufferings, and to touch your heart, that so it may be filled with compassion for them, and with contrition for your sins.

2. The grief of Mary on beholding Jesus.

Mary is anxious to bestow upon her adorable Son proofs of the most faithful love, which never forsakes the beloved object even amid the severest trials. She therefore leaves Jerusalem, and follows her dear Son to Mount Calvary, to be present at His most painful sacrifice of Himself. If you really love Jesus, you should follow Him to Mount Calvary, willingly bearing the Cross of your trials for His sake. Mary also bears her heavy Cross, for she bears in her heart an immense weight of sorrow and suffering, which renders her the most afflicted of mothers. Great, nay, incomprehensible, is her love for Jesus, her Son and her God, and therefore proportionably great and incomprehensible is the grief of her soul on beholding His sufferings. Jesus sympathizes in the anguish of Mary, and Mary partakes of all the sufferings of her beloved Son Jesus, which, as so many sharp swords, rend and transfix her virginal heart. But the most acute pain endured by this afflicted Mother, is caused by the appearance of Jesus when He turns to address the holy woman. How is it, O Mary, that thou dost not die of grief and horror? How is it that thy heart does not break with sorrow? She beholds her dear Son sinking with exhaustion, His Body covered with wounds, and streaming with Blood, His head crowned with thorns, His face defiled with spittle,

His whole adorable Person trembling, powerless and suffering; His neck encircled with a cord, and His shoulders burdened with the heavy and all but insupportable weight of the Cross. She beholds Him overwhelmed with insults by the people, dragged onward by the soldiers, and His sacred Heart bleeding with agony at the sight of her, His sorrowing Mother. "My Son!" would Mary have said, "My beloved Son!" but her excessive sorrow deprives her of the power of utterance. She would willingly draw nigh to Jesus, relieve His sufferings, and enfold Him in a last embrace, but any such comfort is denied her, and she is permitted to give expression to her feelings by tears alone. My soul, contemplate this most afflicted mother, and understand that her sufferings are occasioned by the cruelty with which thou has maltreated Jesus in committing sin. Art thou desirous of diminishing her woes, and of alleviating her bitter sufferings? Bewail thy sins, and never more inflict such torments upon her beloved Son. Compassionate her in her sufferings, and love her as thy Mother.

3. The sorrows of Jesus and Mary at the sight of the sins of men.

Jesus suffers, and Mary suffers, but oh, how far more do they suffer from the sins of men than from all the present and future torments of the Passion! In the insensibility and hardheartedness of those crowds of people who line the road to Calvary, and who behold the sufferings of the Son, and the agony of the Mother, without a feeling of compassion for either, they see an image of the ingratitude of so many Christians, perhaps even of yourself, who never bestow even a single thought or feeling of affection upon Jesus Crucified, and upon Mary the Queen of Dolors. In the insults, outrages, and derisive words heaped upon Jesus in His sufferings by His enemies, they see an image of all those sins by which men will, with equal treachery and barbarity, renew His torments. Oh, what words can describe the sufferings of these two most sacred Hearts! The furious rage with which the Jews are hurrying Jesus to be crucified brings before them in strong colors the mortal sins by which multitudes of souls will, to the end of time, crucify Jesus anew. Alas, that Jesus should have beheld me also on that mountain crucifying Him by my sins! Alas, that Mary also should have seen me; for oh, what a source of sorrows was I to her tender heart! Never more, my soul, never more must thy sins renew the bitter anguish then endured by the adorable Hearts of Jesus and Mary.

THE FRUIT

If you love Mary, never be unmindful of her dolors. If you are desirous of consoling her, save some soul from sin at least by your prayers, and be most careful never to offend her Divine Son. If you wish to please her, imitate her following Jesus in the way of the Cross, by your patience under affliction, and by your pious remembrance of all He suffered for your sake in His painful journey to Calvary.

EXAMPLE

St. Pellegrino Laziosi [St. Peregrine], of the Order of the Servites of Mary, was distinguished by his devotion to Jesus' suffering, and by his tender love and compassion for the Queen of Dolors. Having retired into a cave near Siena, he for a long time passed whole days and nights in the contemplation of these two great objects of his love.

For the space of thirty years he never sat down, having imposed so severe a penance upon himself in honor of the sufferings of Jesus, and of the sorrows of Mary. Our blessed Lord was so well pleased with this devotion of His faithful servant, that He vouchsafed to manifest by a miracle how acceptable it was to Him. The Saint being under the necessity of having one of his legs cut off by the surgeon on account of a gangrened wound in it, the figure of our Crucified Redeemer unfastened itself from the Cross, and, touching the affected part, instantly healed it. (Bollandists, May 1).

DAY 22

The Pious Women Lament over Jesus

MEDITATION

Our Redeemer is followed by a vast multitude of people, and by some women who weep with compassion over His sufferings. Our blessed Lord, turning to them, addresses them in words full of instruction and tender love. Consider—

1. The pious affection displayed by these women.

Crowds of people accompany Jesus, some to insult Him in His sufferings, and some to feast their eyes upon the spectacle of His Crucifixion. Among so many enemies of our Saviour, there are yet a few faithful and compassionate souls who follow Him, and by their tears and sighs give public testimony of the respectful love they bear their suffering Lord. Undaunted by the universal hatred displayed against Jesus by the Jews, undismayed by the rage and malice with which all mistreat the innocent Saviour of the world, they fearlessly stand forward in His favor, and publicly lament over the Just Man, as over a truly worthy object of compassion. Are you one of the few men of faith and piety not afraid of appearing Christians, even where the law of God is disobeyed and trampled under foot? Or do you, on the contrary, yield to cowardly fears, and join the enemies of your Saviour in deriding piety, persecuting innocence and outraging God? On the day of judgment Christ will not acknowledge you if you are now ashamed to acknowledge Him.

The pious women, triumphing over human respect, and overcoming every difficulty, hasten along the road of Calvary to follow Jesus, and render Him the last offices of love and friendship. On seeing Him the victim of such barbarous usage, and covered with wounds and blood, they weep with compassion, and rejoice to offer Jesus the tribute of their tears in return for the Blood which He is shedding so prodigally for the salvation of their souls. Unite in spirit with these pious women, and let your heart be touched at the sight of Jesus covered with wounds, led like a criminal to punishment, and about to sacrifice His life on the Cross. Oh, how sweet and consoling it is to weep

over the sufferings of our dear Saviour. Taste, and
you will see.

2. The favor with which Jesus accepts the
tribute of their tears.

Jesus seeing the compassion felt for Him by
these women, and the tears shed by them over His
sufferings, is pleased to accept and reward the
expression of their love. Learn, hence, how
acceptable is the offering of our compassion and
affection to our suffering Lord, and how sensibly
His Divine Heart is grieved by the ingratitude and
hardheartedness of those who shed not a single tear
over His Crucifixion and Death.

Jesus, although overwhelmed, soul and body,
with the most excruciating sufferings, although
fainting and sinking with exhaustion, is yet
insensible to His own agony, forgetful of Himself,
and occupied solely with the consolation and
instruction of the daughters of Jerusalem. He
beholds their tears, and though He sees that they
spring from an imperfect faith, yet He is pleased
with their humble sorrow, and vouchsafes to reward
them by exciting feelings of love and compunction
in their hearts. He turns to them in the most benign

manner, addresses them in sweet and persuasive accents, and while instructing them in the means of rendering their tears profitable infuses into their souls particular graces and secret inspirations. Thus is Jesus ever good and beneficent in our regard, and ever occupied with our interests. Oh, how many graces would He bestow upon you, if you were but to meditate devoutly upon His Passion! Many tears have you frequently shed over a slight annoyance or illness, or for the death of a friend; but have you ever shed any over the sufferings which Jesus endured for your sake? Perhaps you have never paid Him the tribute of one single sigh. Bewail your thoughtlessness and want of love, and henceforward gratify the Heart of Jesus, to whom tears of compassion for His sufferings are so very acceptable.

3. The words addressed by Jesus to the women.

It is the Will of Jesus Christ that we should compassionate Him in His sufferings, but it is also His Will that our motives in compassionating Him should be similar to His own in dying for us. He suffers on account of our sins, and He desires that our compassion for Him should also have reference

to them. Therefore it is that, turning to the holy
women, He says, *"Weep not for me,* as though I were
going to die for myself, but weep for the cause of my
Passion and death, which is sin. *Weep for yourselves
and for you children,* for whom I am going to die, that
by my death I may make satisfaction for their sins
and for yours." As though He had said, "I praise the
love you have for me, I accept the offering of your
tears, but unless you make reparation for your sins
by tears of true repentance, my Passion and death
will be of no avail to you." "Look at me," says Jesus
to you also, O Christians, "and reflect upon
yourselves, since if I endure such bitter torments for
sins not my own, what eternal punishments must
not be looked for from Divine Justice by those who
neglect to cancel their offenses by tears of true
repentance?" Shed tears of compunction over your
sins which have transformed the Son of God into a
Man of sorrows; your tears will then be of real
service to you, and your compassion for Jesus in His
sufferings will be of lasting benefit to your soul.
They will be blessed tears indeed, if you mingle
them with the Blood of Jesus, and cleanse your soul
from all its defilements.

THE FRUIT

Examine this day which is your most habitual failing, and determine seriously to correct it. Make frequent acts of contrition for your sins, and offer in satisfaction for them the blood shed by Jesus on His way to Calvary. Receive all the trials and tribulations of life as a penance for your sins. You may thus easily pay the debts you owe Divine Justice.

EXAMPLE

Blessed Chiarada of Monte Falco was filled from her childhood with such tender devotion and ardent love for Jesus Crucified, and so eager a desire of suffering, that when only six years of age she would macerate her innocent body by the most excessive mortifications. Her bed was always the bare ground or a hard board. The floor and walls of her room were stained with blood, and bore testimony to the innocent cruelty with which she frequently took the discipline in memory of the sufferings of Jesus. The Passion was the ordinary subject of her meditations, for she would say, "Can anyone who has once beheld Jesus on the Cross ever think of any other object?" Her ardent desire of suffering for the love of Jesus Crucified induced her to implore Him most fervently to give her some share in the pains and torments of His Passion. Our blessed Redeemer appeared to her one day, and told her that her devotion to His sufferings was most pleasing to Him, and that all the instruments of His Passion should be imprinted on her heart; which in effect took place miraculously, so that after her death the wonderful marks were distinctly visible. (See her *Life*).

DAY 23

Jesus is Assisted by Simon of Cyrene to Bear the Cross

MEDITATION

The high priests, fearing lest Jesus should expire from fatigue and suffering in ascending the mountain, take the Cross from His shoulders, and force one Simon of Cyrene, who is by chance passing that way, to carry it for Him. Consider—

1. Wherefore Jesus consents to be assisted in carrying the Cross.

Our Redeemer might, by a miracle, infuse strength into His frame sufficient to enable Him to carry His welcome, long-desired Cross, even to the summit of Mount Calvary. He has already worked other miracles to support sinking nature, and to prevent Himself from expiring at the time of the scourging and during His agony and bloody sweat. He might add this one more to the number. But such is not His will. It is His will to have companions to bear the Cross with Him. It is His will that others should feel the weight of His Cross, and this is why He sinks down and requires assistance, and not because He is weary of bearing His Cross, or that He finds its weight insupportable. His consent that another should relieve Him of His Cross arises from no desire of unburdening His sacred shoulders, but is a mystery intended to teach us that He is pleased to share His sufferings with all His elect. On the other hand, Jesus is, at the same time, ready to bear His Cross so long as to fall several times beneath its weight, and even finally to expire upon it. And with what degree of constancy do you bear your Cross? Do you persevere in virtue? Are you firm and constant in your resolution to follow Jesus Christ, and to suffer with Him and for Him? Remember that whoever does not take up his Cross and follow Jesus, is not worthy of Him. Whoever has not partaken of His sufferings will not partake of His glory. Jesus desires to associate us with Himself in His eternal happiness, and for that reason it is His will that we, in the person of Simon of Cyrene, should assist Him to carry His Cross. Therefore, if it is cruelty on the part of the Jews to relieve Jesus of His burden, only because they desire to see Him die the death of the Cross, on His part it is love for you, zeal for your salvation, and a burning desire to make you partake of those sufferings by which He is meriting eternal glory.

2. The happiness of the Cyrenian in being chosen to assist Jesus in bearing His Cross.

Among all the multitude of people following Jesus Christ to Mount Calvary, not one man offers to assist Him in bearing His Cross. All look upon it with horror as a public mark of infamy. Not one of the many disciples and friends of our blessed Redeemer will risk his reputation so far, or has courage sufficient to relieve our suffering Jesus of the heavy burden beneath which He is sinking. Oh, how many there are in the world who call themselves followers of Christ, but, the moment an opportunity offers of suffering anything for His sake, take to flight, make excuses, and declare themselves, by their actions, the enemies of the Cross of Christ! Are you one of these? Remember that to bear the Cross with Christ is not a counsel only, but an obligation for all who wish to save their souls. While the Jews are seeking for someone to carry the Cross of Jesus, they fall in with a stranger from the city of Cyrene, who is passing that way, and him they force to take up the Cross. Thus is this man singled out by Providence to be honored with bearing the Cross of Jesus. How fortunate is he in being able to relieve our dear Redeemer of His burden! What a happiness to have to ascend Mount Calvary in His company—to partake of His sufferings, His ignominy, and His fatigues! What an honor to bear this Cross, which has been already so tenderly embraced by Jesus, and sprinkled with His Divine Blood! My soul, if thou hadst been in the place of Simon of Cyrene, and hadst known who and what Jesus was, as thou knowest now, wouldst thou not most willingly have assisted Him to carry His Cross? Wouldst thou not have considered it a happiness to bear that heavy Cross upon thy own shoulders, to relieve the agonizing Son of God? Most certainly thou wouldst. Well, if thou bearest thy trials patiently, if thou dost struggle generously against thy temptations, thou wilt enjoy an honor similar to that of the Cyrenean. All our sufferings are portions of the Cross of Jesus. They have all in the first instance afflicted His blessed Soul and Body. He has experienced all the sufferings which you now endure. He has borne the sorrows which afflict you. You will diminish the burden laid on Jesus, you will relieve His sufferings, if you bear your Cross willingly and joyfully for love of Him. Promise our sweet Jesus that you will do so from this moment.

3. In what manner a Christian should bear the Cross.

The Gospel does not say that Simon of Cyrene refused to take up the Cross he was required to bear, or that he murmured or lamented over his fate. Behold the example which you should follow. The crosses of our own choice are good, but those sent us by Providence are better, from whatever source they may proceed. To accept them in silence, receive them without complaint, and bear them with patience, will rend them meritorious, and make us true followers of Jesus Christ. Simon of Cyrene bears the Cross after Jesus, keeping Him always before his eyes.

Oh, how joyfully should we suffer did we always keep Jesus Crucified before our eyes! When we contemplate Our Saviour covered with blood and wounds, expiating our sins in His own Person, at the price of so much suffering, how willingly do we bear our cross, how willingly do we bear our cross, overcome our depraved appetites, resist our evil inclinations and avoid sin! Every Cross seems light, all sufferings easy, when we bear them in union with Jesus. Endeavor then always to remain united to Jesus in your sufferings.

Finally, Simon of Cyrene bears the Cross of Jesus to assist and relieve Him, and bears it even to the summit of Mount Calvary. How many persons bear the Cross, feel all its weight, and faint from fatigue, but derive no advantage from it to their souls, because it is not the Cross of Jesus that they are bearing. They suffer, but for the world; they suffer, but to content their own whims; they make the most painful sacrifices, but for anything rather than the love of Jesus. No merit will you ever have in your sufferings unless you suffer for the sake of Jesus. Neither will your sufferings ever be rewarded if you persevere not to the end in suffering for Jesus. You must follow Jesus even to the summit of Mount Calvary, that is to say, with fidelity even unto death.

THE FRUIT

The crosses imposed upon men by the world are not found heavy, because men love the world. Love Jesus Christ, and you will patiently bear the crosses He sends you. Everything that is painful to the flesh, disagreeable to the senses, or displeasing to self-love, is a Cross. Embrace all these little opportunities of suffering, and you will be bearing the Cross of Christ. Refuse not to relieve the poor and afflicted for the love of Jesus, and He will accept as given to Himself whatever consolation or assistance you charitably bestow upon your suffering neighbor.

EXAMPLE

Blessed Veronica Giuliani, who from her earliest childhood was most devout to the Passion of Jesus Christ, and who, when in her novitiate among the Capuchinesses, was filled with a very eager desire of suffering for His sake, was one day ordered by her mistress to carry water to the infirmary. Now there were two flights of very steep stairs to be ascended from the place where the water was drawn, to the infirmary, and the servant of God, whose fervor knew no bounds, carried up more than thirty pitchers full, so that her feet were dreadfully galled, from the number of times she had to ascend and descend the stairs, and she was completely exhausted and ready to faint. While she was in this state our Divine Redeemer appeared to her, bearing His Cross, and said, in touching accents, "Look at the Cross which I am bearing; observe how heavy it is." At this sight the soul of the blessed novice leaped for joy, so that she felt her strength restored, and her heart burning with eagerness to suffer yet more for the love of Jesus. Imagine that Jesus addresses the like words to you when oppressed with weariness, and you will experience their virtue. (See *Life*).

* * * * *

You would do right also to meditate on the precious gift given us on Veronica's Veil. By uniting his suffering to that of Jesus in His Passion, the Christian is able to wipe from the Precious Face of our Lord the tears, the sweat, the Blood. The soul then becomes the veil that reveals to the world the majestic countenance of the Suffering Servant, whose majesty is His Love!

[Publisher's note]

* * * * *

DAY 24

Jesus Nailed to the Cross

MEDITATION

Jesus having reached the top of Mount Calvary, the Jews will not allow a moment's delay, but most barbarously and cruelly fasten Him with nails to the Cross. Consider—

1. The sufferings of Jesus before His Crucifixion.

Jesus has arrived at the end of His journeys on reaching the summit of Calvary, but He has not attained the termination of His sufferings, which henceforward become truly unmeasured. His enemies throng around, while each and all freely insult and curse Him as a malefactor, who now at last is to suffer the penalty of His crimes. The Divine and patient Victim remains perfectly silent, and fixing His eyes and thoughts upon the Cross, contemplates the scaffold upon which He is soon to yield up His last breath, and joyfully offers up His life as a sacrifice for the salvation of mankind. Jesus suffers in every part of His agonizing frame, save in

His tongue, but He permits not this member to continue longer without its share of torment. It is the custom to give all condemned criminals about to be executed some refreshing and comforting beverage. But even this last office of humanity and compassion is not fulfilled towards Jesus Christ in His state of utter exhaustion and suffering, and the soldiers barbarously offer Him wine mingled with bitter gall, to torture His palate and stomach. Such is the beverage which you have presented to Jesus by your evil habits, censorious and pretended piety, sensual pleasures, and innumerable sins. They are the bitter gall which you have offered to your Lord, even when He was quenching your thirst with the sweet waters of His love and goodness. Now, at least, offer your suffering Redeemer the refreshment of your tears—tears of sincere sorrow and tender compassion. No sooner has Jesus tasted the bitter and disgusting liquid than the executioners strip off His garment with cruel violence. My soul, look on thy Saviour, and compassionate Him in these new sufferings. Owing to the quantity of blood and the countless wounds which cover His sacred Body, the garments had again adhered to His lacerated flesh, so that on their being torn off, all His wounds are re-opened, and His sufferings become quite indescribable, while the Blood flows to the ground in streams. Oh, see how Jesus sheds every drop of His Blood for your salvation! And thou, my soul thou for whom thy Saviour sheds such torrents of blood, thou for whom this Man of Sorrows endures so much, wilt thou not shed one tear, nor breathe one sigh for all His sufferings? Wilt thou be hardhearted toward thy Crucified Jesus alone?

2. The obedience of Jesus in placing Himself upon the Cross.

The Cross is already lying on the ground, the altar is prepared on which the adorable Victim is to ascend to be sacrificed. The executioners command Jesus to lie down upon the Cross, and the instant He receives the order, in deference to His Divine Father, He bends His knees, reverently bows down His Head, and wishing to be obedient even to the most ignominious of deaths, lies down on that hard bed of suffering and infamy. By this great act of disobedience does Jesus make satisfaction for the disobedience with which we have so often violated the commands of God. See, my soul, see how Jesus manifests no repugnance to obey the cruel order. There is no need of employing force to make Him obey it. He willingly, and of His own accord, stretches Himself out upon the Cross, places His lacerated and bleeding Body in the proper position, presents His hands and His feet to be nailed, and raising His eyes to Heaven offers Himself in sacrifice to His Eternal Father for the salvation of the whole world, and even of my poor soul, fervently beseeching Him to pardon our sins through the merits of His obedience. You who are so willing to obey the commands of the world, of the flesh, and of your own concupiscence, and on the other hand so stubborn and rebellious to the law of God, what can you say on beholding this most wonderful example of obedience in the Son of the Most High? How many excuses, difficulties, and pretexts do you bring forward by way of exempting yourselves from the observance of the law? You are creatures, why then refuse to subject yourselves to the commands of the Creator? You are servants, why then disobey the ordinances of your celestial Master? To teach you the important virtue of obedience, Jesus has subjected Himself even to the ignominious death of the Cross. Can it cost you as much to obey God as it has cost Jesus to obey His Divine Father for the salvation of your soul?

3. The sufferings of Jesus in His Crucifixion.

Jesus having stretched forth His hands on the Cross, as though to fold all sinners in His embraces, and reconcile them with God, the executioners fasten them to the wood with large nails, by dint of violent and repeated blows of a heavy hammer. These nails pierce entirely through, tearing and crushing flesh, nerves, veins, arteries, and all that make any resistance. Inexpressible are the sufferings of our blessed Jesus, and so great is His agony that He is all but ready to expire from utter exhaustion and intense anguish. In the meantime, the Blood of our sweet Redeemer, that Blood which He is offering to His Eternal Father for me, flows forth in copious streams. Harder than a rock must your heart be, if you are not moved to tears at so mournful a spectacle. Draw nigh to Jesus and reverently ask Him what are those wounds in His hands and feet, and He will answer that they are the work of your sins and the pledges of His love. He will tell you that, to cancel your sinful deeds, He has allowed His most sacred hands to be pierced through with nails. Read then in these wounds the history of your sinfulness, and detest it, read in them the history of His love, and be grateful for it. The hands of our dying Redeemer being nailed to the Cross, the same torture is inflicted on His feet. By reason of the violence with which the executioners stretch His Body, and the cruel manner in which they strike and hammer the large nail that is to transfix both feet, Jesus endures unspeakable torture, and asks you to afford Him some consolation by shedding at least one tear of compassion, or breathing one sigh of affection, at the sight of His sufferings. Will you refuse that much to Jesus, who asks for it from His Cross? See with what patience, meekness, and silence He endures the most excruciating tortures, without uttering one word of complaint, either of the nails which so painfully tear His flesh, or of the executioners who treat Him as inhumanly as though He were the worst of malefactors. He is your Leader whom you must seek to resemble, if you desire to save your soul. What resemblance do you bear to Jesus, you who lead a delicate, sensual life—you who are passionate and impatient under the slightest suffering? Ah, my sweet Jesus! I adore thy precious wounds, and through their merits do I implore grace to imitate Thee.

THE FRUIT

Renew this day your determination of obeying God at any cost, and of ever preferring His Divine Will before all else. Whenever you feel any repugnance to obey man for the love of God, remember the obedience with which Jesus Christ submitted to the commands of His executioners themselves. Make it a rule to dwell frequently each day in the wounds of Jesus often paying them homage by acts of adoration and love, and taking refuge within them in all dangers and temptations.

EXAMPLE

The remembrance of the most painful Crucifixion of Jesus inspires the heart of a Christian with love for God and desire to suffer for His sake. Blessed Christina of Spoleto was one day meditating upon the sufferings of Jesus, and the point she was considering happened to be the dreadful wound made by the nail in the feet of Jesus. "Oh, ungrateful wretch that thou art!" she said to herself, "behold how much Blood He has shed for love of thee; and what has thou done to prove thy love and gratitude for such infinite goodness?" So saying, being filled with holy fervor, she took a large nail from the wall, and pierced her feet entirely through with it, too happy thus to return Jesus blood for blood, and wound for wound. Jesus asks not so much of you, but at least you may inflict some penance for love of Him upon your hands, which have committed so many sins, and upon your feet, which have taken so many steps in the paths of iniquity. (Bollandists, 14th Feb.). That you may frequently call to mind the wounds of Jesus Christ, imitate the example of the venerable Father Alphonsus of Orosco, an Augustinian monk, who was accustomed, whenever he heard the clock strike, to remember the blows of the hammer nailing down the feet and hands of Jesus. (See his *Life*).

DAY 25

Jesus Elevated on His Cross in the Sight of All

MEDITATION

The executioners having fastened Jesus with nails to the Cross, raise Him in the air between two thieves in the presence of all the people. Pause awhile, and gaze upon your dying Saviour, with deep compassion and earnest devotion. Consider—

1. His bodily sufferings.

The vibration of the Cross when raised in the air reopens the wounds of that torn and lacerated Body, thus inflicting tortures of the most acute nature upon our blessed Jesus. Raised thus on high, and hanging on three nails, our dear Lord rests solely upon the deep and momentarily increasing wounds of His hands and feet. In this state, the thought alone of which makes us shudder, does Jesus pass the last three hours of His life. Oh, what anguish, what indescribable, incomprehensible sufferings, does Jesus endure in so painful a situation! And ought not this consideration to arouse in you feelings of the deepest love for that goodness and charity which has induced Him to ascend the Cross, and endure such countless sufferings for love of you, to heal your infirmities, and save you from Hell? How hard must your heart be, if you are not touched by such a spectacle! There is not a single portion of the Body of Jesus, from the crown of His head to the sole of His foot, that can be called whole, and that has not its own particular suffering, as He hangs upon the Cross. His head is crowned with thorns, and He has not where to lay it; His adorable face is defiled with spittle, and overspread with the pallid hue of death; His eyes are bloodshot, His flesh lacerated, His bones may be numbered, His hands and feet are pierced with nails, and every part of His Body is torn and streaming with blood. My soul, behold the Blood which, when applied to thee in the Sacraments, has so often cleansed thee from thy sins! Behold the wounds which thy sins have so frequently opened afresh! Behold the condition to which the Son of God, thy Father and Saviour, is reduced for love of thee! Behold what excruciating sufferings He is enduring to make satisfaction for thy sins!

2. The opprobrium with which He is overwhelmed.

The insults and opprobrious words with which Jesus is loaded, equal the excessive sufferings He endures in His Body, and, before His death, He is truly satiated with them. The Jews, having crucified two thieves together with Him, elevate Him on the Cross between them in the sight of all the people, that so He may appear as the worst malefactor of the three. Oh, with what confusion must the Son of God, the Holy of Holies, have been overwhelmed on beholding Himself thus shamefully dishonored before so large a multitude! What deep sorrow must have filled His sacred Heart on seeing His good name and honor thus infamously vilified and degraded! And yet, our suffering Lord submits to everything with the most admirable patience and unexampled meekness. Behold what your pride has cost Jesus, since to cure it in you, and make satisfaction for it, He has endured such terrible infamy.

His enemies, not yet satisfied, and being devoid of every feeling of humanity, insult Him in His sufferings, mock Him, and load Him with curses and blasphemies, deriding His patience, and defying Him in insulting language, *to come down from the Cross!* All mock and reproach Him, and vie with one another, by the most insulting gestures and language, in making Jesus truly the outcast of the people, and satiating Him with outrages. What pain must such disgraceful insults have occasioned the Heart of our innocent Lord! He sees His enemies all rejoicing and triumphing at His sufferings. He might in one instant have struck them dead, and thus have proved Himself to be the Almighty God, suffering and dying only because such is His will. And yet our most meek Lord, with unshaken fortitude, submits to be thus dishonored, without expressing the slightest emotion of anger, and without answering a single word. He beholds His honor attacked in its most tender point, and He well knows the evil intentions with which the Jews are insulting and deriding Him, yet He shows no resentment, but suffers in humility and silence. Learn from such an heroic example not to resent the evil that is done you, not to indulge in anger, nor to revenge the injuries you receive from others. How can you call yourself a Christian, if you do not

imitate the example left you by Jesus Christ on the
Cross?

3. The acute interior anguish of the Soul of
Jesus.

The exterior sufferings of our Blessed Redeemer
are occasioned by the hatred of His enemies, but the
interior sufferings of His Soul are caused by His love
toward you. So excessive are they, that of them
alone, out of all His tortures, does our Saviour
mildly complain to His heavenly Father. Jesus might
sweeten His sufferings, as He has since sweetened
those of His martyrs; but it is His will to drink the
bitter chalice of His Passion without any alleviation
or comfort; it is His will to die plunged in an abyss
of mortal anguish, weariness, sadness, and affliction,
and with His holy Soul overwhelmed with sorrow.
And if He receives any consolation from the
Divinity to support Him through His Passion, it is
only that He may suffer the more. Understand now
at least what mortal sin is, since, in order to make
satisfaction for it, a God-man dies thus immersed in
a sea of sorrow. The circumstance of His most
blessed Body being exposed naked before the eyes
of all, is a source of great confusion to Him. Deeply

also is His Soul afflicted at beholding Himself
placed between two thieves, and at hearing the
disgraceful epithets and derisive words showered
upon him. The hatred, ingratitude, and
hardheartedness of His beloved people grieve His
merciful heart. Your want of love, your ingratitude
for all His charity, the manner in which you have
abused and trampled His Blood underfoot,
overwhelm His sacred Soul with bitter sorrow. His
blessed Soul is soon to be separated from His Body
by the most infamous and ignominious of deaths,
and His infinitely precious life is about to be
sacrificed like that of a malefactor upon a
disgraceful Cross. Oh, deep and inexpressible,
indeed, is the interior anguish of Jesus! And yet He
accepts all, willingly suffers the whole bitterness of
His most dolorous Passion, and offers it up on the
altar of the Cross to His Eternal Father for the
salvation of mankind. And will you not joyfully
sacrifice such or such a passion, or burst of anger, or
guilty friendship, for the sake of your soul and out
of ingratitude to Jesus? For the love of Him who for
your sake submitted to the painful separation of
soul and body, will you not fly forever from such or

such an occasion of sin, or such and such objects of your attachment, which absorb affections due solely to your most loving Lord? Ah, yes, otherwise too great would be your ingratitude toward Him who has suffered so much for you!

THE FRUIT

Whenever you meditate, or look upon the Crucifix, say to yourself, *"Behold the condition to which my sins have reduced the Son of God!"* and make acts of repentance and confidence in His mercy. When tempted to commit any sin, direct your thoughts to Jesus hanging on the Cross, and say *"Jesus Crucified! And I about to commit sin? Can this be? Never! Never!"* There can be no remedy more efficacious against temptations of the flesh than the remembrance of the humiliations and sufferings endured by Jesus on the Cross. Let such be your habitual thoughts, that you may avail yourself of them to some purpose when you stand in need.

EXAMPLE

Our Divine Saviour appeared once to St. Bridget in the state in which He was when nailed to the Cross, all covered with the Blood that was streaming from His wounds. The Saint being overwhelmed with sorrow at such a sight, exclaimed in a transport of love, "Ah, Lord! Who has reduced Thee to so mournful a condition?" "Those," replied the Saviour of the world, "who despise My law, and, unmoved by all I have suffered for them, repay My love only by ingratitude." So deep an impression did this vision make upon the heart of the Saint, that she could never think of the Passion without shedding floods of tears. The bleeding form of her Saviour was ever present to her mind; wherever she was it was always before her eyes, and when at work the abundance of her tears frequently forced her to pause. She was most ingenious in finding out methods of afflicting and macerating her flesh in memory of the sufferings of her Redeemer. She had a wound in her body, which she reopened every Friday, dropping burning wax upon it, thereby to nourish in her heart a lively remembrance of the sufferings of Jesus. Learn from this Saint frequently to remember the Passion of your Saviour, and to practice some mortification for His love. (See her *Life*).

Day 26

Jesus Crucified Prays for His Enemies

Meditation

Our Divine Lord, hanging on the Cross in the sight of the assembled multitudes, insulted, scorned, blasphemed by His enemies, turns to His Eternal Father, and beseeches Him to *forgive them, for they know not what they do.* Consider—

1. The Charity with which Jesus prays.

After a prolonged period of silence, our dying Saviour at length opens His lips, to teach us the most sublime lesson of love from the pulpit of the Cross. It is the first time that Jesus has spoken from His Cross, and the first words He utters are to implore pardon for His enemies, whilst they are in the very act of most barbarously depriving Him of life. He forgets all His own sufferings in His solicitude to apply a remedy to the spiritual wounds of His executioners. Not all the bitter torments He is enduring cause Him such exquisite pain as the thought of their damnation. He remembers not by whose hands His sufferings are inflicted; He

remembers only for whom He is dying, and He
procures the eternal salvation of His very crucifiers!
Sin is hateful to Jesus; He is dying to destroy it; but
the sinner is most dear to Him; He is dying for his
salvation, and in death is only desirous of affording
proofs to His persecutors of the inscrutable depths
of His love for them. Then, turning to His Divine
Father, "Most beloved Father," He exclaims with His
dying accents, "to Thee I offer this Blood, these
wounds, this Cross, to move Thee to pardon My
enemies, who have inflicted upon Me so cruel a
death." Oh, surprising charity! The thought of the
eternal perdition of the souls of His crucifiers is a
greater source of suffering to Jesus than His own
most bitter Passion! He is expiring in the most
excruciating torments, and in death implores grace
and pardon for His murderers! Can we conceive
more burning love than this, which is neither
extinguished nor damped by even the overflowing
waters of boundless sorrow? Truly this is a sublime
lesson of what your conduct towards those who
injure or offend you should be. How can you have
the heart to desire to revenge yourselves upon your
enemies, when Jesus, with such tender charity, is

solely occupied with obtaining the pardon of those who have crucified Him? Very possibly your enemy may not deserve that you should pardon him, but the Blood and Wounds of Jesus Crucified have merited that you should grant that pardon for His sake. The slightest feeling of hatred entertained against your neighbor wounds the loving Heart of Jesus, and is an obstacle to the remission of your own sins.

2. For whom Jesus prays.

Not only does Jesus pray for those who are crucifying and blaspheming Him, but He likewise prays for all sinners, for all who have contributed to His sufferings and death. May not the most wretched sinners take courage at the thought of this prayer of Jesus? For in it He includes not merely His executioners, accusers, and judges; that is to say, not only the Jews who so clamorously demanded His death, but all sinners without exception, since all who have committed sin have thereby been the cause of His death. Yes, my soul, every time that thou hast sinned thou hast renewed the cause of the death of the Son of God, thou hast crucified Him anew; and by every fresh sin thou committest thou renderest thyself guilty of His death. And shall not sin, which has crucified Jesus, be henceforth most hateful to me? But oh, how sweet and how deserving of love must be my Divine Jesus, who prays for me, even whilst I am desiring His death! Ah, sweet Jesus! in the very height of Thy sufferings, in Thy mortal agony, Thou art mindful of sinners, Thou art mindful of me! Are not even my innumerable sins and base ingratitude sufficient to banish me from Thy loving Heart? Are not all my sins present to Thy mind, being as they are the very cause of Thy death? And still Thou dost implore Thy Eternal Father to forgive me! But through the blessed effects of that prayer, Thy death, which is caused by my sins, has become my hope and my salvation. Art thou a sinner? What canst thou fear, when Jesus Christ Himself is the Great Advocate who prays for thee, and from His Cross beseeches His Father to pardon thee? Come, come, O sinner, cast thyself with entire confidence at the feet of Jesus, bathe them with thy tears, and then, if sincerely penitent, thou wilt be secure of forgiveness and Heaven. But if thou persistest in sin, His Blood will be thy condemnation.

3. The excuse alleged by Jesus in His prayer for His enemies.

Jesus might have taken awful vengeance upon His enemies from the Cross, and exterminated them in one moment from the face of the earth; but He prefers exhibiting Himself in the character of a God of peace and mercy, and giving proof of the most tender solicitous charity. To move His Father to have compassion on those who are insulting and deriding Him by the most impious expression of scorn, He seeks to excuse and palliate their guild by saying that *they know not what they do.* They have given free vent to their hatred of His sacred Person by the most atrocious calumnies; they have consummated the most fearful injustice by crucifying Him; they are even now seeking to load Him with contumely by their insulting gestures and derisive words; and yet Jesus in His infinite charity pities and excuses their sin, and fulfills the loving office of an Advocate by having recourse to Divine clemency in their behalf. He hides their wickedness beneath the torrents of His own Blood, and implores His Father to accept the excuse of their ignorance, willful though it is, in attenuation of their guilt and malice. Oh, how great is the clemency and goodness of God our Redeemer! Such, my soul, is the lesson taught thee by the example of thy dying Saviour. Not only shouldst thou forgive thy enemy, or whoever has done thee an injury, but thou shouldst also do him all the good in thy power, pity and excuse him, and desire that he may one day attain the possession of eternal happiness. Ah, what would become of me, had Jesus entreated me as I treat my neighbor, when, for a slight injury or affront, I resolve to be avenged, and indulge in thoughts of hatred and anger? My most sweet Jesus, I beseech Thee to enkindle in my heart the flames of a charity like unto Thine, which may teach me how to love and pity every one who does me an injury. I love my neighbor for Thy sake. I forgive all who may have offended me from the bottom of my heart; and I beseech Thee, O Father of mercies, to cancel their debts, and shower forth Thy graces upon them.

THE FRUIT

Imitate Jesus praying from His Cross for His enemies, if you wish to have any part in the pardon He then sought to obtain for you. Be reconciled with your brother if you wish to make your peace with God. Delay not, for if you are obstinate in sin, you will die impenitent. Excuse those who persecute you; suffer in silence; forget and forgive. Hate sin, but not the sinner, because for him did Christ die, and for him did He sacrifice His life.

EXAMPLE

A glance at the Crucifix is a powerful incentive to the pardon of injuries. St. Philip Neri, finding the most tender and urgent solicitations of no avail in persuading a certain young man to pardon an injury which had been done him, took a Crucifix, and said with great earnestness, "Look upon this image, and remember how our Divine Lord shed the last drop of His Blood for love of thee, and how on His Cross He prayed to His Eternal Father for the very men who had crucified Him!" The young man was struck by these words, and far more by the sight of Jesus on the Cross. He trembled all over, and answered with many tears, "Behold, Father, I am now most willing to pardon every injury, and to make all the reparation that lies in my power." If you feel any difficulty in pardoning an injury, imagine that Jesus implores you from His Cross to forgive it for love of Him. (See *Life of St. P. Neri*).

Day 27

*Jesus from His Cross bestows Mary upon us as our
Mother*

Meditation

1. The hour of the death of Jesus is fast
approaching, and He beholds from His Cross His
most dear and loving Mother, who is standing at its
foot, assisting at His last sufferings in deep but silent
agony, and He would address her for the last time.
Bending down His sacred head, turning His dying
eyes towards her, and indicating by a glance His
beloved disciple, John, His pallid lips breathe forth
the words, *"Woman, behold thy Son;"* by which He
bestows all the faithful in the person of John upon
her as her children. Such loving solicitude evinced
for her by Jesus at this last awful hour is some
consolation to Mary, but oh! what new anguish fills
her heart on hearing that we poor sinners are given
her in the place of Jesus the Man-God, and that she
is to receive us as children in His stead! Her most
amiable, beloved, and holy Son Jesus is taken from
her, and ungrateful, wicked men, His crucifiers,

given her in exchange! Oh, how deep is the anguish of her immaculate heart! She is desirous of replying to the words of her Divine Son, or of addressing John, but at that very moment she feels her maternal heart overflowing with new love, and with the deepest emotions of charity she accepts as her children the faithful of all ages in the person of the beloved disciple John; "for these, O woman," whispers a secret voice, "these shall be thy children." She beholds them at this time deformed with sin, the enemies of God, and objects of His wrath, nevertheless she accepts them! Oh, great indeed is the goodness of Mary, who, with tender and compassionate love, then receives her new children, and embraces them with all the loving solicitude of a Mother. Then, O Mary, even so ungrateful a sinner as myself has been given to thee as a child, and received by thee as such! How can my heart ever testify sufficient gratitude to thee, or be filled with love and veneration commensurate with thy charity! O happy sinners, remember what a Mother you have, remember whose children you are! Your Mother is Mary, the Mother of God; a Mother full of grace, a Mother the mirror of purity and holiness. It is not fitting that so holy a Mother should have sinful children. Are you desirous of being her true children? Fulfill the obligations of children in her regard, and never grieve her maternal heart by your hateful sins.

2. Jesus, then addressing John, and indicating Mary by a glance, says, in loving accents, *"Behold thy Mother."* As though He had said, "By My death thou does lose thy Father, but behold I leave thee My Mother in My place; I bestow her upon thee and upon all the faithful in thy person, that you may all regard her as your Mother." Jesus is not satisfied with saying to Mary, *"Behold thy son* in the person of His beloved disciple, John;" but He also addresses these words to John: *"Behold thy Mother,"* that the gift being reciprocal, the sentiments of love and confidence may be reciprocal too. Oh, how great is the gift bestowed upon us by Jesus in this His last will and testament! Our dear Saviour has nothing else on earth to leave us but His own most holy Mother. His Body He has delivered up to the fury of His enemies, His Blood He has shed for the redemption of the world, His garments the soldiers have divided amongst themselves; nothing therefore

remains for Him to bequeath, save His most blessed
Mother, and her He leaves to John and to all
Christians in his person. He bequeaths this tender
Mother to us at the very moment when her soul is
pierced by a double-edged sword of grief, and her
heart distracted between anguish for the death of
her Son, and desire for the salvation of men. O most
amiable Redeemer! how precious is the legacy
which Thou leavest us in the last hours of Thy life.
Whilst Thou art expiring, overwhelmed with
ignominy and suffering, Thou dost bestow upon us
the happiness of having Thee for our Elder Brother,
and Mary for our Mother. I humbly beseech Thee,
since Mary is my Mother, to give me grace to regard
her as such, and to serve and love her with all the
tenderness of a true son.

Take courage, devout soul, lift up thy eyes to
our Crucified Jesus, listen to His voice, and hear
how lovingly He says to thee, "Son, *behold thy
Mother.*" Look at this Mother with the tenderest
feelings of affection, and know that Jesus has placed
in her hands all the blessings His mercy is willing to
bestow upon us. No one is saved but through Mary,
no one receives any blessing but by the hands of

Mary, no one obtains pardon but through the intercession of Mary. Gratefully acknowledge the goodness of Jesus, have recourse with confidence to Mary, and let thy conduct be that of a son in her regard.

3. Thus enriched by the possession of so great a treasure, John, having in the name of all the faithful accepted Mary as a Mother, takes her to his own home after the death and burial of Jesus, bestows upon her all the anxious care due to a parent, and respects, honors, and serves her with the most filial devotion.

Similar are the duties which you must also fulfill as a child of Mary. You must entertain for her sentiments of profound respect, tender love, and filial confidence, and your desires and inclinations must ever be conformable to hers. She is the Mother of Purity and Queen of Virgins, and it is by purity of heart and morals that you will please her. Her whole life never displayed anything but holiness, innocence, and purity; and she will ever bestow upon you her most loving protection and particular patronage, she will ever be to you the tenderest of Mothers, if, in imitation of her, you lead a pure, holy, and innocent life. You will experience the effects of her maternal love if you are in all things a docile and devoted child. Listen how she says to you from the foot of the Cross, where she is sorrowfully attending the last agonies of her dying Son, "Behold, I am your Mother." Look at her suffering on account of those sins which have crucified Jesus, and weep at the sight of the bitter anguish with which they have filled her heart. Promise never more to commit those sins which crucify her Son anew, and cause her to be the most afflicted of Mothers. Sweet Mother! through that inexpressible sorrow which thou didst suffer at the foot of the Cross on account of my sins, obtain for me grace to be henceforward a dutiful child to thee, and never more by my sins to become guilty of the death of thy most amiable Son Jesus; obtain for me grace to love thee constantly, to serve thee with the utmost fidelity, and to honor thee with heartfelt devotion, so that through the merits of the death of Jesus, and thy own deep sorrow, I may one day attain the happiness of praising and blessing my God and thee eternally in Heaven.

The Fruit

Next to Jesus, let your whole confidence be given to Mary, and suffer not one single hour of the day to pass without having recourse to her. But your devotion to Mary must mainly consist in delighting her pure heart by your love of modesty, purity, and humility; virtues so inexpressibly dear to hear. You will never be really devout to her, unless you try to please her; and an impure, contaminated, proud heart never can be pleasing in the eyes of the Mother of Purity. In your endeavors to acquire the virtues of humility and modesty, let it be your intention to imitate the most blessed Virgin, and you will be fulfilling the duties of a son in her regard.

Example

St. John Nepomucen was the child of prayer, for it was through the intercession of the blessed Virgin, to whom his parents had had recourse, that a son was granted to their fervent and earnest prayers. The name of John was bestowed upon him in honor of that disciple to whom Mary was given as a Mother by Jesus. And truly did Mary show herself a Mother to him, for she obtained his recovery from a

dangerous illness in his childhood. As John grew
older, he faithfully fulfilled every duty of a true
child of Mary, for he tenderly and fervently loved,
honored, and served her, and in every necessity she
was his sweetest refuge. Being tempted by King
Wenceslaus to break the sacred seal of Confession,
and threatened with death on account of his
persevering refusal to accede to so impious a
request, he undertook a pilgrimage to a venerated
shrine of his dear Mother, there to implore her
assistance in the assaults to which he was exposed.
Mary did not fail to assist her faithful servant, and
obtained for him such signal graces that, when his
constancy was again put to the proof, he triumphed
over every temptation, and, in consequence, was put
to death; thus terminating a life which had been
wholly employed in the love and service of Mary by
a glorious martyrdom. (See his *Life*). Accustom
yourself in all temptations to have recourse to Mary,
and you will experience the effects of her
intercession.

DAY 28

*Jesus Crucified complains of being forsaken by His
Eternal Father*

MEDITATION

Towards the ninth hour, that is to say, after having
been three hours upon the Cross, our dying Jesus
cries out with a loud voice, *"My God, My God, why
hast Thou forsaken me?"* Consider—

1. What does Jesus intend to teach us by this
mournful cry of complaint?

In all the bitter torments of His Passion, Jesus
has never uttered a single word of complaint, but in
the last moments of His life He cries out with a loud
and mournful voice, that we may understand that
His exterior and interior sufferings have now
reached their utmost height. What man is there so
hardhearted as not to compassionate our dying,
suffering Redeemer? Not one complaint has He
uttered in the midst of all His torments, but now,
when about to die, He reverently complains to His
Divine Father, *"Why hast Thou forsaken Me?"* to make
known to us the excess of anguish which He is

enduring at being thus forsaken, and that all mankind may be fully aware of the inexpressible sufferings which the salvation of our souls has cost Him. Oh, how much are we indebted to the tender love He bears us! Jesus complains, not that He is forsaken by the Divinity, nor that the Eternal Father is divided from His most beloved Son; but as man, that His suffering humanity feels as though destitute of help or consolation, and, as it were, plunged into a sea of inexpressible sorrow, that to all it may be made known that, God though He is, His sufferings are not thereby alleviated or diminished in the slightest degree, but rather increased and rendered more acute; also, that we may understand how terrible must be the rigor of Divine justice, which requires that He should be abandoned to all the fury of His enemies, to endure every imaginable torment, and, finally, to undergo the most ignominious and cruel death of the Cross. This inexpressibly painful feeling of dereliction, which thus elicits a complaint even from the Son of God, is the shadow of the sufferings experienced by the damned in Hell, when in the midst of their torments they are, moreover, conscious that they are hated by God, who was once their Father, but is henceforward their most implacable enemy. This last thought fills up the measure of their eternal fury, anguish, and despair. Implore your sweet Jesus never to deprive you of His grace in this world, that so you may not incur the dreadful misfortune of being eternally forsaken by Him.

2. The painful effects of this dereliction.

Almighty God usually bestows upon martyrs delightful alleviations of their sufferings, by infusing into their souls sweet interior consolations, so that they rejoice in torments, and go to meet the most cruel deaths exultingly. But Jesus, amid all His sufferings, is deprived of any consolations to temper the bitterness of His anguish. His soul is steeped in all the bitterness that has been or ever will be experienced by the martyrs, and yet is left without the slightest consolation. Jesus, whilst enduring the dereliction, has to taste the whole bitterness of the chalice of His Passion without one drop of refreshing sweetness. To the exterior sufferings which He endures in His whole Person, in His body, head, hands, and feet, are added the interior torments of mental agony, sorrow, fear, sadness, and

most terrible desolation of spirit. All these
sufferings, which have been most acute during the
whole course of His Passion, reach their extreme
height on Mount Calvary. Thus does Jesus become
in very truth the Man of Sorrows, the King of
Martyrs, and the Most Afflicted of Men. My soul,
canst thou meditate upon the excessive sufferings
endured by the most holy Soul of thy dying
Redeemer, and not be enamored with His
unbounded love in thus submitting to them for thy
sake? Art thou not moved even to tears of
compassion when thou rememberest the part thy
sins also have had in inflicting the pangs of
martyrdom upon His most loving Heart? Knowest
thou of what Jesus complains most bitterly on the
Cross? To see that His Blood, His Passion, and Death
will be of avail but to few! He laments and grieves at
the sight of the small number of those who will
profit by the Blood which He sheds so lavishly for
all. This is the source of the deep sorrow which
oppresses and overwhelms the Heart of Jesus. O my
dear Redeemer! permit not that I should ever be one
of that numerous host of reprobates, who, by their
own fault, render Thy Passion and Death of no avail.

Grant, sweet Jesus, that I may never be separated from Thee by accursed sin, and that I may one day come to enjoy in Heaven the blessed effects of Thy Death which has merited it for me.

3. The sentiments of Jesus in His dereliction.

Jesus Christ, although abandoned by His Father to the mercy of His most furious enemies, to the whole bitterness of His torments, and to the most ignominious death, nevertheless casts Himself entirely, and without reserve, into the arms of this same beloved Father. He had taught us how to live; on the Cross He teaches us how to die. His whole Soul had always been absorbed in God; He had ever been entirely resigned to the Divine will, and had reposed with the most perfect trust in the arms of His Father. At the moment of death, He yields up His Spirit to God, and commends it to the all-merciful Providence of His beloved Father. Imitate Jesus in life and in death. Live so as to be able to say with perfect confidence at the hour of death, "*Into Thy Hands, O Lord, I commend my spirit.*" In the meantime, accustom yourself often to yield up to God your body, your soul, and all you possess. He is our Father, and the very best of Fathers: He cannot forsake us. Our names are inscribed on His loving Heart, and He never can forget us. His hands have formed these bodies of ours, and from Him have we received our souls, which He created to His own image. There is nothing that can be denied us by a God who has given us His own beloved Son, and delivered Him up to death for our sakes. Often remind Jesus of all that your soul has cost Him, and beseech Him to save it; recommend it to His Heart transfixed with a spear, implore Him to watch over it, never to abandon it, and, above all, to preserve it from sin, and bestow upon it the gift of His love.

THE FRUIT

When you are deprived of all consolation or comfort in misfortune or suffering, reflect that Jesus is bestowing upon you some small portion of that anguish which He endured in His dereliction, thus to render you more like unto Himself. Be not discouraged, faint not, if you experience no sensible pleasure, but rather a feeling of repugnance, in the service of God. Look at Jesus suffering on the Cross, and let this sight be your sweetest encouragement and best incentive to perseverance in those works of piety which you have undertaken for the love of God.

EXAMPLE

Devotion to the most sacred Passion of Jesus is a mark of predestination. Blessed James of Bevagna, a Dominican friar, was most devout from his earliest childhood to Jesus Crucified, and being one day disturbed by an importunate feeling of fear concerning his eternal salvation, threw himself in a suppliant posture at the feet of his suffering Lord, to pray for grace and consolation. Jesus lovingly spoke to him from the Crucifix, saying, "This Blood, O my son, shall be to thee a mark of predestination;" and at the same moment so copious a stream of Blood flowed from the Crucifix as to bathe the whole face and dress of the blessed man. So great a favor filled his heart with a sweet feeling of confidence that he should be saved, and with an earnest desire of loving his Crucified Lord more and more, and of being for ever united to Him in Heaven, a happiness to which he afterwards, in fact, attained. (See his *Life*).

Day 29

Thirst of Jesus on the Cross

Meditation

1. The last moments of our dying Redeemer are at hand. His throat being parched, and His whole Body consumed with inward fever, owing to the immense quantity of blood He has lost, and the innumerable tortures and sufferings He has endured, He exclaims in a mournful voice, "*I thirst!*"

Long has He suffered this thirst, and patiently has He forborn to utter a word of complaint; but yet, when now at length He reveals it, even in the tone of a suppliant imploring relief, there is not found one man who will give Him a drop of water to refresh His burning lips! The God who created the rivers, and supplied the sea with fountains of water; the God who miraculously assuaged the thirst of a million of Jews in the desert;—that God is without even a drop of water to moisten His parched lips! Thus does our Divine Saviour expiate in His own Person our gluttony and excessive delicacy! Thus does He endure the penalty of the sins we commit

by our intemperance in eating and drinking. A
soldier now raised to the mouth of our Lord a
sponge soaked in vinegar. Can you point out any
culprit treated with such refinement of cruelty as
this exercised upon the innocent Son of God in the
midst of His most excruciating sufferings? My soul,
compassionate thy sweet Jesus. He says, "*I thirst*,"
and yet they do not even give Him a drop of water
to moisten His lips! But little does God require of
you to satisfy His Divine Heart, and yet you refuse
Him even that little! At what time does Jesus say, "*I
thirst*"? When about to die, when plunged in an
abyss of suffering, when about to consummate His
great sacrifice for our redemption! At what time do
you refuse God the little He asks of you? At the very
moment when He is most liberally loading you with
benefits of every description! Oh, how great is your
ingratitude! From whence does Jesus say, "*I thirst*"?
From the Cross, on which He has been languishing
for three long hours. The very place from which He
speaks ought to be sufficient to move you to
compassion. At the sight of a God hanging for your
sake upon a Cross, and imploring you to correct
some fault, break off some improper friendship, or

fly from some occasion of sin, can you turn away, can you refuse Him that consolation? Ah, reflect at least before uttering a refusal which will be a source of so much suffering to Him!

2. Besides this corporal thirst, Jesus suffers from another spiritual species of thirst, which cannot be so easily assuaged.

Jesus thirsts for our eternal salvation, He thirsts for souls. This is the thirst of which he complains, and which is consuming His very life's Blood. Jesus most passionately desires that the Blood He has shed should benefit mankind by saving them from Hell; and yet He foreknows that there will be many eternally lost, notwithstanding all His love and all His sufferings. Oh, truly does this thirst consume the loving Heart of Jesus, and its sacred heat slowly but surely deprives Him of life!

My soul, reflect now what things thy desires tend to, and what thou does thirst after. No doubt thou thirstest after worldly goods, after honors, pleasures, comforts, and amusements, but thou thirstest not after thy salvation; thou are not desirous of gaining heaven, of entering into the possession of that eternal, undying bliss which Jesus has purchased for thee at so dear a rate. Jesus Crucified thirsts in an especial manner after thy salvation and progress in Divine love. If thou hadst been present on Mount Calvary, and hadst heard our Redeemer saying, "*I thirst,*" wouldst thou not have relieved His sufferings by giving Him a little water? Know that even at the present moment it is in thy power to relieve His burning thirst. He says to thee from the Cross, "My Son, *I thirst* for thy soul." Art thou desirous of affording thy Redeemer some solace in His sufferings from thirst? Offer Him thy thoughts by frequent consideration on His goodness and sufferings. Give Him thy heart with all its affections by constant protestations that thou lovest Him above all things, and will ever love Him in preference to all created objects. Give Him thy soul with all its powers, and often renew thy resolution to work out thy eternal salvation, however much it may cost thee, and hope that thy efforts may be crowned with success, through the merits of His Passion. Thus mayest thou relieve Jesus in His thirst.

3. Consider a third species of thirst endured by Jesus.

The thirst to suffer yet more for the glory of His

beloved Father, and the salvation of souls. Jesus has drunk the bitter chalice of His Passion, even to the dregs, and yet He thirsts to suffer even more for love of us. Be filled with admiration at the ardent charity of Jesus, which causes His sacred Heart to be consumed by such a thirst of love, and thank Him for His great goodness in suffering so much for your sake, and desiring to suffer yet more. There can be no doubt but that Jesus would have prolonged His bitter sufferings, had not the will of His Father disposed otherwise, so great was the love He bore your souls. Are you filled with a thirst of labor and suffering for the love of Jesus? Do you thirst with a desire to struggle and fight manfully to save your soul? Perhaps your thirst is the thirst of the world, the flesh, and earthly goods, a thirst which overwhelms the Heart of Jesus with bitterness. Jesus loves His Eternal Father with an infinite love, and rejoices that, for His greater glory, His body is slowly consumed with suffering, and that His spirit continues to drink the bitter chalice of fresh afflictions. He rejoices that His sacrifice is prolonged through every species of ignominy, in order to honor His Father, and that His life is slowly departing

amidst agony and suffering, that so His obedience to
the Divine will may be yet further exercised, and
His beloved Father more and more glorified. Now
cast a glance upon yourself. Do you joyfully endure
the sufferings with which life is strewn? Do you love
God in the midst of your trials? Do you kiss the
hand which chastises you? Do you desire to glorify
God by the sacrifice of your patience? Do you thirst
for God to be honored by yourself and all others?
Do you thirst after the performance of good and
virtuous actions, which alone can give satisfaction
and joy to the Heart of Jesus? Examine yourself, and
resolve to amend.

THE FRUIT

The remembrance of the thirst of Jesus on the
Cross, and of the gall and vinegar given Him to
drink, should serve you as an incentive to
mortification of the palate, and as a lesson in
sobriety and temperance. Dwell in thought upon
your past life, and bitterly deplore that you have so
often given Jesus gall and vinegar to drink, by your
sinful deeds. Entertain a most earnest and
persevering desire to save your soul, and thirst

eagerly after that eternal Fountain of life which is prepared for you in Heaven.

EXAMPLE

The faithful followers of Jesus Crucified willingly deprived themselves, for His love, of even the most innocent gratifications that creatures can afford them. One day in the height of summer, Saint Paul of the Cross was returning with a fellow-religious from a mission which he had been giving, and, owing to the extreme heat of the weather, he was suffering greatly from thirst, when suddenly they came to a clear fountain of water, which seemed to invite them to drink. The servant of God turned to his companion, and said to him, smiling, "Shall we now perform an act of mortification by abstaining from this water? For the love of Jesus enduring such burning thirst on the Cross, let us make a sacrifice of this gratification of our palate." His fervent companion immediately assented to the proposal, which was forthwith acted upon. This act of mortification was so pleasing in the sight of our Divine Lord, that He speedily rewarded His servant by abundant spiritual favors. (See his *Life*).

DAY 30

Jesus dies on the Cross

MEDITATION

Jesus, after having commended His Spirit to His Father, after being three hours on the Cross in agony of body and desolation of mind, at length bows His head and dies. Consider—

1. Who is it that dies?

He is the Son of God, the only begotten of the Most High, who is immense and infinite in all His adorable perfections. He is the God of Glory; God most loving, most holy. The ocean of all good dies for thee, a creature most vile, most wicked, a sink of every vice, a sea of miseries, a monster of ingratitude. So it is: the Creator dies for the creature; the Lord for the servant; God for man. And art thou not struck with wonder at seeing a God dying for thee, solely on account of the love He bears thee! Where is thy emotion, where is thy astonishment, at the sight of such a death, such condescension! *A God has died for man.* This thought was the sweetest, this reflection was the most endearing, to the saints. This was the powerful motive to the love of God. *A God has died for man.* This is the suggestive of the confusion and despair of the damned in Hell. "A God has died for me," will the damned soul exclaim, "and yet I burn, I despair in those flames. I cannot doubt of His love, if He has died upon the Cross to save me. Therefore if I am damned, it is all through my own malice." Ah! deservedly does that soul burn eternally who has been ungrateful and frowardly heedless of a God Crucified and dying for man. My soul, wouldst thou rather burn for ever in the unquenchable fire, than burn now with the love of that God who has died for thee on the Cross? And is it possible that, after having beheld God dying for thy love, thou wilt not cease to offend Him, to maltreat Him, to despise His tender charity? Draw near, my soul, to the foot of the Cross, where cold and bloodless hangs the Body of thy dead Jesus; repent of thy past ingratitude; thank Him for having died for thee, and freed thee from eternal pains; put thy trust in His Blood, and in His sacred Wounds, and promise Him never more to draw thyself away from His love.

2. How does He die?

He dies, after having poured forth in cruel anguish all the sacred Blood in His veins. He dies, satiated with insults, with reproaches, and ignominies. He dies, plunged in an ocean of inexplicable pains and torments. He dies consumed, not so much by the raging fire of His sufferings, as by the living furnace of His charity. Which of us can wish to live except in order to love our Jesus? Which of us would like to suffer except in order to give Him pleasure? Who will dare to make Him die over again by accursed sin? Jesus dies, bowing his head in sign of obedience and submission to his Eternal Father. He could have prolonged His life, and even abolished death altogether, but He was pleased to die, and allow the force and atrocity of His pains to slay Him, in order that His obedience might reach to death itself. By His obedience He repairs the damages caused by the first fatal disobedience; He restores to the Divine Majesty the honor that had been robbed, and puts man again in possession of Paradise. God does not require of you an obedience that will cost you your life; yet how remiss are you in obeying? It may be, indeed, that the observance of some precept will cost you something. But will you not obey God, your Lord, your Sovereign Lord? Will not you, a vile creature, do this, seeing Jesus has obeyed even unto death? Jesus bows His head towards us, to express the lovingness of the invitation He gives us to approach Him. But, ah! who accepts so sweet, so loving an invitation? How long is it since Jesus invited you to penance? How often has He entreated you to come and ask pardon? And do you defer coming to One who is so anxious to receive you! Shall you, to satisfy a wrong desire, delay to approach Jesus calling you from the Cross? Resolve this moment to amend.

3. Where does He die?

He dies on the Cross, suspended by three nails, between two thieves, covered with wounds, in the presence of an immense multitude. Behold the excess of a God loving. One sigh, one tear of His, would have been sufficient to redeem the world. That would not satisfy the love of Jesus. He wished for death—the death of the Cross. Fix thy gaze, my soul, upon the adorable lifeless Body of thy Jesus, which still hangs from the Cross. See this beautiful countenance, pale, livid, defiled with blood and spittle; this head pierced with thorns; those hands and feet perforated with big nails; those members rent and torn until the bones may be numbered. At the sight, the sky is covered with heavy darkness, the earth is shook, all creation emits a voice of sorrow and mourning. How is thy heart moved towards its good God, its dear Father, its loving Brother, just expired for your sake? The number of Wounds opened in His sacred Body are so many mouths which speak and preach of love. Canst thou doubt of being loved by Jesus? Canst thou live without making a return? My soul, thy value is the life of a God. Thou owest thy life to the Son of God, who gave His for thee on the Cross. What enormous injustice would it be if thou gavest thy love to the world, to the flesh, to the devils, thy cruel enemies, and deniest it to Jesus? O my Jesus! I am no longer mine, nor do I wish to be another's, but only Thine, who hast died for me, and Thine I wish to be for eternity. My soul has cost Thee much. Grant that I may know its value, that I may esteem it, and no longer give it away to sin and the devil. Grant that I may spend the remainder of my life in serving Thee and loving Thee with all my heart.

The Fruit

Look often at your Crucifix, and say with affectionate devotion, *"A God died on the Cross for me."* Kiss often His sacred feet, bathing them with tears of true contrition. The Crucifix will be the only object of comfort and consolation that can be presented to Thee at the hour of death. Try now so to act that the love and the Wounds of Jesus serve not to reproach thee at that terrible moment.

Example

Devotion to the sufferings of Jesus procures us a holy death. The blessed Joachim Piccolomini, of the order of Servites, having had during life a tender devotion, and kept up a loving remembrance of the Passion of our Lord, and not having had the opportunity of shredding his blood for Him by martyrdom, begged earnestly of the blessed Virgin to procure for him the privilege of dying on Good Friday, in order that he might thus have, at least, the happiness of giving up his life on the same day on which Jesus laid down His upon the Cross. The loving Mother was pleased at the petition. On the very day he prayed for, whilst assisting at the function, and the Passion was being sung, he was buried in the thought of the pains and sufferings of Jesus Crucified, and just as the words, "He gave up the ghost," were pronounced, he sweetly rendered his soul up to his Maker, by a death which excited the wonder and holy envy of all present. (*Annal. De Serv. Mariae*).

Day 31

The side of Jesus wounded by a spear

Meditation

Our blessed Saviour having expired, a soldier, more cruel and impious than the rest, imagining that He may yet be alive, wounds Him in the side with a lance. Consider—

1. The cruelty displayed towards Jesus on this occasion.

The barbarity of the enemies of Jesus is not satiated by all the inhuman tortures inflicted upon His living Body, but, more cruel than death itself, they turn their rage against the sacred Body of their dead Redeemer. A man, however wicked he may have been, is an object of compassion when once he has given his life in expiation of his crimes. The outrages offered to Jesus alone are endless, the insults heaped upon His sacred Person alone are unlimited. Jesus is already dead, why then open His side with a lance? Why is not the hatred borne Him by the Jews at last extinguished? Why is their cruelty not yet satiated by all the sufferings which have been inflicted upon their innocent Saviour? Behold how that sharp lance, directed by eager hands, inflicts a deep wound upon the breast of Jesus, and pierces through and through His adorable Heart. Oh, cruel spear! But oh, far more cruel hands that direct it! How frequently have you, O sinner, not merely crucified Jesus anew by sin, but persisted in wounding and lacerating His most holy Heart over and over again by your continual offenses! Repeatedly have you thus cruelly and impiously outraged your loving Redeemer. How many times have you re-opened that wound? Detest your malice, bewail your ingratitude, and cleanse all the stains wherewith your soul is defiled, in that Blood and water which issues from the side of your Redeemer.

Jesus feels no pain from the wound at the moment of its infliction, but He suffered it by anticipation, and by the knowledge He had of the atrocious cruelty of the man who would inflict it; still He willingly accepted this indignity, and submitted to so barbarous an outrage. Jesus spares not Himself in any way where the salvation of your soul is concerned, whereas, oh, how ungenerous and niggardly are you in His regard! Ah, such is not the manner in which you should correspond with the infinite love of Jesus, who has deigned to suffer for your sake with so much generosity!

2. The love displayed by Jesus for us.

The Son of God was not satisfied with giving us proofs of His love during life, but it was His will to give us additional proofs of it even after death. It was His will thereby to show us that His love was not quenched by death. Therefore He permitted that His sacred side should be opened with a spear after His death, so that we might behold His divine Heart pierced for love of us. Thus was a door opened to us, through which we might enter, and behold the ever living, ever burning love of the Heart of Jesus, even after death. His sufferings might deprive Him of life, but not of love, which, like a mighty fire, burned more brightly and clearly still, when fed with the fuel of sufferings. Do I desire to increase in love for Jesus, I need but fix my eyes upon Him as He hangs dead on the Cross for love of me, and behold how His sacred Body has been lacerated and immolated for my sake. Those wounds which bleed no longer, because every vein is emptied of the last drop of its blood, tell us loudly how great, how excessive, is the love of God for us, since it has reduced Him to such a condition for our sake. But why add a fresh wound to that lacerated Body, from which the soul is already separated? Oh, truly precious wound! inflicted by reason of the excessive charity of a God, whose desire it is to make known to us how great, even after death, is His love for man. His Heart is a furnace of love, which not all the waters of the sea can ever extinguish. Oh, is there any one to be found, who can contemplate that open side, that tender, wounded, loving Heart, without feeling himself obliged to return love for love? Enter, my soul, enter into the burning furnace of the tender Heart of Jesus, enter it frequently in spirit, and there thy incredible hardness of heart will be softened, and thy icy coldness warmed; thou wilt be inflamed with holy love for thy God. Behold the last drop of warm Blood issuing from that sacred Heart, and bathing the soldier who has inflicted the wound! The scourges had not drawn that last drop, neither had the thorns, or the nails, but now, at last, the spear opens it a passage, and it flows forth! O surprising and excessive charity of Jesus! Who gives even the last drop of His Heart's blood, and gives it for the good of those who inflict the wound upon Him! And are you so fearful of bestowing too much upon Jesus, if you bestow all your love upon Him, that you are obliged to share it with a thousand vain objects? Permit me, O my Jesus, to kiss Thy wounded side, and to enter into Thy Divine Heart, where Thou mayest destroy my malice in the flames of its charity, transform me totally into Thyself, and fill my soul with Thy Divine love.

3. The mystery therein represented.

From the side of Adam asleep, the Almighty took a rib, of which He formed Eve, the mother of all the living, thereby representing in figure what would be accomplished in the death of Jesus. The death of our Redeemer is but the sleep of the Second Adam, the Repairer of the evils brought upon the world by the first. Therefore, whilst He is sleeping the sleep of love upon the Cross, His side is pierced by the lance, in order that the Church, His beloved Spouse, the Mother of all the faithful may come forth from His side, that is to say, from His adorable Heart. Behold of how great a Mother your faith makes you the happy son! She derives her existence from the most pure Heart of a Man-God. Must not your origin be Divine also, since you are the son of such a Mother? What therefore can be more suitable, since you derive your existence from the most loving Heart of Jesus, than that you should return whence you came forth, and should be unable to find true rest or happiness, save in the Heart of your Lord? From that wounded Heart has likewise flowed the water which sanctified you in baptism, and which has so often cleansed you from your sins in Confession. Comprehend, if possible, the price, the value, the dignity, and merit of holy Baptism, and the excellence of the august title of a Christian, which it bestows upon you. Through it, you are born again to a new life of grace, you are put in possession of the precious inheritance of the sons of God, you acquire a right to the eternal inheritance of Heaven, you become one of the people of God, the brother of Jesus Christ, His co-heir, and a member of His mystical Body, the Church. So numerous, therefore, are the favors, so noble the prerogatives, which you derive from the wounded side of Jesus! What gratitude do you feel towards your Divine Redeemer for blessings so great and innumerable?

Have you ever even thought of them with the slightest emotions of gratitude? How often have you thanked your Lord for His infinite goodness and mercy? Strange as it may seem, it yet is a fact, that Christians live and die without having perhaps once returned God thanks for so extraordinary a favor as that of being children of the true Church of Jesus Christ, or having even considered the grace of being Christians as any extraordinary favor! Value so great a happiness as it deserves, and be grateful for it to Jesus, through whose wounded Heart it has been bestowed upon you.

THE FRUIT

Consecrate yourself this day to the love of the sacred Heart of Jesus—the center of all hearts. In all your trials and temptations, take refuge in the side of your Redeemer, endeavoring to make most fervent and lively acts of love for His adorable Heart. Return God thanks every morning and evening, for the singular favor He has bestowed upon you in making you a Christian, and a member of His Church. Glory in being, in appearing, and in professing yourself a Christian on every occasion.

Do not disgrace the august and venerable character bestowed upon you in Baptism, by committing sin, or by leading a life unworthy of a Christian.

EXAMPLE

Blessed Francis Lippi, a Carmelite friar, was most devout to the Passion of Jesus Christ, and accustomed to spend several hours each day in meditating upon it, with many tears. It happened one day, that being engaged in this pious exercise, and considering how excessive were the sufferings of his Jesus on the Cross, and how great was the cruelty of those who pierced His side with a spear after death, he wished that his eyes might be changed into two fountains of tears, that so he might weep unrestrainedly over the sufferings and outrages endured by his loving Redeemer; when, behold! there appeared unto him Jesus nailed to the Cross, covered with blood, and His side pierced with a spear. The following words were then addressed to him in a voice faint with exhaustion: *"Behold, O Francis, how much I have suffered for the love of man, and what an ungrateful return he yet makes Me for all My sufferings."* The vision then disappeared.

At this mournful spectacle the blessed man wept bitterly over the sufferings of his sweet Jesus, and, taking an iron chain, scourged his body severely, until he had made his blood flow in streams for the love of Him who for his sake had shed even the last drop of His own, and he meanwhile exclaimed in sorrowful accents, "It is I, O Lord, it is I who am the cause of Thy sufferings; it is I who am the cause of Thy bitter Passion!" (See his *Life*). Repeat these or similar words whenever you look at the Crucifix.

Other publications by Jacob Stein:

Saint Gabriel of Our Lady of Sorrows: Collected Writings

Explanation of the Holy Mass
and
Praying the Mass: During Advent
both from the writings of Dom Gueranger

Special thanks to:

My brother, Justin,
Mr. Johnnatan Ibarra,
Mr. Christopher Pujol,
Miss Selina Fang,
Miss Ann Barnhardt

and

my family and friends

for their contribution and support
with these initial publications.

Please say an Ave for their intentions.

Made in the USA
Las Vegas, NV
27 January 2022

42427583R00135